HARMONY OF THE UNIVERSE

HARMONY OF THE UNIVERSE

THE SCIENCE BEHIND HEALING, PRAYER AND SPIRITUAL DEVELOPMENT

by

ANDREW GLAZEWSKI

Edited by
Paul Kieniewicz

www.whitecrowbooks.com

CONTENTS

LIST OF FIGURES

Andrew Glazewski at Attingham Park, ©1968

ACKNOWLEDGEMENTS

This work could not have been undertaken without the support and encouragement of Andrew Glazewski's family, his nephews and nieces who loaned me tape recordings and correspondence left after his death. The Wrekin Trust, Radionics Association and the British Dowsing Society kindly permitted the reprinting of several of Andrew's papers. John MacManaway of the Westbank Healing Centre provided me with tape recordings of Andrew's talks left by his father, Bruce MacManaway. Ruth Nesfield-Cookson generously shared with me her memories of her long friendship with Andrew and copies of his papers. Marjorie Bloomfield provided me research material of her late husband Bob Bloomfield, including tape recordings of conversations with Andrew's brother Konstanty. Bradstreet Stewart of the Sacred Science Institute provided the rare illustrations from the works of Hans Kayser. Thanks also to Ann Procter, Ann and Roger Wharmby and Ben Ashton for help with copying and restoring tapes, to Isabel Cowan for help with editing the manuscript. And to former residents of Ilford Park for sharing their memories.

EDITOR'S FOREWORD

Father Andrew Głażewski (1905-1973) is still remembered by surviving parishioners at Ilford Park, as a kind priest who fulfilled the duties expected of him: to marry the young, bury the dead, administer sacraments and preach sermons. Few of them knew anything about his scientific work, the study of the field that surrounds plants, crystals, animals and people. One parishioner who had known him for over twenty years, admitted that she had no idea that he was a physicist or that half of his living space was occupied by a laboratory of magnetic coils, electrostatic generators and machines whose function only he understood.

"He was also a healer," I said.

"I guess he healed someone somewhere," she replied. "He said many, strange things."

Outside his parish, a small enclave of Polish exiles in southern Devon, he was known as a mystic, scientist and healer. He didn't care if English speaking people, who couldn't pronounce his name, called him "Glass of Whisky" though he insisted that he wasn't all that "spiritual." He preferred to be addressed as Andrew—without the Father or other title. But the Poles, a traditionalist people still used: Father, Canon, Very Reverend or Father Canon Deacon.

He appeared in my life when I was thirteen and like Tolkien's Gandalf, sent me on a quest as strange as that of Bilbo Baggins, and then quietly disappeared eleven years later. Forty years after his death, people talk about him, as an extraordinary person who changed their lives. Through lectures and workshops he taught meditation, and healing through interaction with the human field. After his death his healing technique was continued by others. It is most similar to Therapeutic Touch developed by Dolores Krieger, Dora Kunz and others, and now practised by hundreds of nurses throughout the United States and in the UK.

Since 1945, when Andrew first discovered that he could heal, often over large distances, he set about developing a scientific theory to explain it. Rejecting ideas about fantastic, unknown forces of nature, he focused on the known fact that the human body generates an electric, infra-red and sonic field. He also drew on the work of Gustav Stromberg, the Swedish astronomer who published papers on a field-oriented physics, and the musical theorist Hans Kayser. For forty years Andrew developed this theory and perfected his healing technique. He built a laboratory in which he tested his ideas through experiments. He published the results in a few early papers. Unfortunately he never published important details on the practice of healing. Such advice was given only in talks, workshops or to those who worked closely with him.

After Andrew's death other writers have developed the biological field theory, most notably Rupert Sheldrake who applied the theory to explain diverse phenomena as inheritance, the formation of crystals, learning and consciousness. Both Sheldrake and Andrew Glazewski derived their theory from the same historical sources.

However Andrew's teaching is much more than theoretical physics whose testing is limited to laboratories with expensive equipment. Anyone who takes the trouble to train him/herself in healing can test it. It also formed the basis for Andrew's spiritual life and for his understanding of the spiritual worlds. Using the language of physics and fields he described angels, spirits and even God.

Alongside his work on the science behind healing, Andrew carried out his duties as the parish priest to the Polish exiles with great energy. Many of his parishioners, conservative Catholics who didn't believe in anything they couldn't see or touch, found his teachings impenetrable. Though he tried to speak to them in a language they understood, he could not speak as a traditionalist. He shared his spiritual vision in all his sermons, whether or not anyone understood it.

"You're not your body," I heard him say to his parishioners during a Mass in 1971. I was amazed that he even tried to raise the subject. "Your body is only a radio transmitter. You are not the radio, but the radio waves that exist far beyond your body. You are the field that surrounds your body. You're only conditioned to believe that you're inside your body. Your body is actually inside you. And with practice, you can change your point of view to that of the field. That's the real you. After you die, you won't be lying in any grave."

Despite sermons that they couldn't relate to, the parishioners all loved him. They'd never known a priest who was so special, though no one could say what that "special-ness" amounted to. The parish children all loved him. They looked forward to their Saturday religious classes, more nature outings than indoctrination. Every summer he held a summer camp on the Scilly Islands for the young people of the parish. To this day they remember those camps fondly.

On November 2, the traditional All Souls Day procession in the Newton Abbot cemetery still begins at his grave.

"He was a very kind man," a parishioner told me. "Going to him for confession was more of a treat than to be dreaded. He treated penitents with great respect, always had sensitive advice that left them feeling a lot better about themselves. Each Mass he said was, well different. It drew you in."

I first met him in 1962 when he gave a Lenten retreat at Divine Mercy College, the boarding school I was attending near Henley on Thames. He led retreats on two other occasions. Instead of talking to us about leading a good or godly life, he taught us about human psychology, how to unblock ourselves and reach our fullest potential, about healing, angels, and how to meditate without words. Surprisingly we didn't hear a lot about God. Years later when I was a university student our paths crossed again. We struck up a correspondence that grew into a close friendship.

Andrew was born in 1905[1] in the family home on the banks of the Dniester close to the Ukrainian village of Chmielowa. It had been the home for the Głażewski's for generations. They were landed gentry, somewhat well off. In those days many Polish families owned large tracts of property in the Eastern Reaches (Kresy, Pol). They regarded themselves as Polish. That Poland did not exist as a political entity made no difference. The Polish language, religion and history were preserved in each family. Andrew grew up with two older brothers, Konstanty and Gustav, and Ignacy his younger brother.

When the First World War broke out, the rural country became too dangerous, on account of roving paramilitary groups, and so the family moved to Lviv. During his teenage years Andrew attended the local school in Lviv. He also devoted his efforts to the piano. He learned the piano by ear, and had few formal lessons and yet developed his skill to where he could play complex pieces, practising often eight hours a day. Perhaps he dreamed of becoming a concert pianist. Ignacy Paderewski, the composer and piano virtuoso who later became Poland's first prime minister, supposedly gave Andrew some lessons.

When the time came for him to enrol in university, he chose to study law. His father insisted on it as a way to develop a successful career. He also paid for the studies.

Andrew entered the University of Lviv in 1923, immersed himself all aspects of university life—the parties, dances and the girls. In any social situation he was the life of the party, with a cockiness that everyone admired, a sharp intellect and quick tongue. He was a good dancer, especially of the Mazur. In the drawing room, he could dazzle people with his piano playing. He was also an excellent figure skater and accomplished in many of the complex moves of figure skating.

"So when did you decide to be a priest?" I asked him in 1972 while we were walking on the Scillies.

He looked away thoughtfully, then said, "My decision came upon me very quickly. In the space of half an hour."

It took place in 1925 during a sermon in a Carmelite church. The Mass was in celebration of Thérèse of Lisieux, who had just been pronounced a saint. The Carmelite sisters held a three day period of prayers. Andrew's mother, Adela encouraged Andrew to attend the event.

"I first became aware of spiritual worlds when I was eighteen," he told me. "I was in an empty street when I heard voices—many of them, surrounding me. They were clearly voices of people who weren't visible, but they were there."

By the time his calling came upon him, he was confident enough in his spiritual perception to know that he had to follow it. The spiritual world was already very close to him, visceral, something that was not an article of faith but something that he could touch.

Andrew's father insisted that his boy finish his law degree, and then think about his spiritual vocation. The sudden conversion of the boy who loved parties and women seemed incomprehensible. And so Andrew continued with his law studies. However at the end of the year he failed, of all subjects, Latin. His father, influenced by Andrew's mother, finally dropped his opposition and allowed him to pursue his vocation.

At first he joined the Dominican order. Dominicans were known as foremost theological scholars, a subject already of great interest to him. In his later life Andrew said that many of his discoveries on the science behind healing had their basis in the writings of Thomas Aquinas, the eminent thirteenth century theologian.

He soon found out that life with the Dominicans was too physically demanding. Dominicans practised an austere discipline. During winter the rooms were unheated. Novitiates had to kneel on bare stone, sleep on cold stone. After one year Andrew realized that he could not endure the austerities. He never had a strong physical constitution. Of all the brothers, he was the weak and gangly one who tended to get sick.

After leaving the Dominican order he enrolled in the novitiate in Lviv to become a secular priest, and was ordained in 1931. At first he was assigned as vicar to a small church, but he wanted to continue his theological studies. He enrolled at the University Angelicum in Rome. Run by the Dominican Order, Angelicum was established in the early thirteenth century as a leading theological university. In 1265 Thomas Aquinas became regent of the college

His studies in Rome left time for other activities too. He moved in Polish aristocratic circles, was a frequent guest at the Polish embassy. At Rome he also reconnected with a close family friend, the artist Jan Rosen. Rosen was commissioned to paint the ceiling for the Pope's private chapel at Castel Gandolfo, a battle scene in which the Poles defeated the Red Army. Requiring a model for the priest who, crucifix in hand, led the Poles into battle, Rosen asked Andrew to model for him.

Other than theology, Andrew studied physics and became familiar with the current discoveries of the atom. He felt that science had to be an active partner of theology, that God worked within the framework of the laws of nature and not outside them. Even apparently miraculous healings had to have their basis in unknown natural laws. He set himself the task of discovering those laws.

He returned to Poland where he was assigned a small parish near his hometown. But he was not there for long before the Second World War broke out. Soon afterwards, the archbishop of Lviv asked Andrew to go to Rome as an emissary because Andrew had made many contacts there, to present an issue to the Vatican. The three Catholic congregations in the city, Roman, Armenian and Ruthian had to take a stand on the legality of the Russian invasion, but they could not make any official statement without word from the Vatican. Andrew departed for Rome. He had to deal with thick snow in the Carpathian Mountains as well as being arrested by the Romanians after dodging the Russians. After he had finished his task in Rome, he was advised by a Polish Bishop not to go back to Lviv; but to proceed to France where he could join up with Polish forces currently being mobilized. This he did, and became a chaplain with the rank of Captain in the Polish army.

After the collapse of France in 1940 he crossed over to England. He was assigned as chaplain to the First Rifle Brigade, located near Cupar. However the lull in the storm that surrounded Britain was short-lived. Soon he was called back to active service. His deliberations about the non-physical world would have to wait.

Following D-Day, he was assigned as chaplain to the 10th Mounted Rifle Regiment and sent to Europe. He soon found himself in the thick of battle. He was wounded twice. For his efforts he later received the Polish Cross of Valour twice and the Silver Cross of Merit with Swords.

There's no doubt that he saw the human slaughter at close quarters, experienced scenes that psychologically unhinged many others, at the least left emotional scars that never healed. However Andrew appeared unaffected by the conflict.

After the war was over he returned with his army unit to England to serve as chaplain to soldiers in the Grimsditch Resettlement Camp near Salisbury. The situation there was difficult, with soldiers awaiting demobilization, at loose ends, uncertain of what the future might bring, in full knowledge that they could not easily return to Poland.

His life took a major turn when he discovered that he could use his hands to heal. It's likely that he first discovered that ability on the battlefield. Many healers discovered their power in a crisis situation, such as a battlefield, where there were many seriously wounded comrades, and medical help was far away.[2]

He looked for answers in the phenomenon of dowsing, and found to his surprise that he was able to dowse for water. That the divining rod twisted in his hands as if it had a will of its own. Hoping to meet others who might be able to explain the phenomenon, he joined the British Society of Dowsers. This proved an inspired move as he met George De La Waar and Cecil Maby, both experimental scientists and well-known dowsers with whom he was to later collaborate.

In 1948 he was assigned to Ilford Park Resettlement Camp. Located in a disused military base near Newton Abbott, it became known as "Little Poland", the home to almost a thousand Polish refugees, many seriously wounded, both physically and psychologically and who were unable to integrate into British society. He remained there as their chaplain until his death in 1973.

Upon moving into his quarters, a long barrack with a curved roof of corrugated iron, he established his laboratory in the unoccupied section. He was certain that a study of the human field would yield the explanations that he sought. He accumulated a vast library of scholarly texts on music, physics and mathematics. He conducted regular measurements of the Earth's magnetic field. His experimental work ran in tandem with his theoretical studies, combining concepts from atomic physics, gravitation and music. The sheer amount of work, leading to three scientific papers, suggests that his scientific work overshadowed his pastoral work. But he didn't see them as in conflict. He knew that a study of natural law would lead him to understand the mind of God.

Forty years after his death, my memories of him remain vivid, especially the summer of 1972 that we spent together on the Scillies. I can still see him standing by the campfire, a small pendulum dangling from his hand, twirling madly like a Tibetan prayer wheel. Or walking through the grass to the tent where he celebrated Mass every day at 4pm. The air about him was still. He was focused on his task with a seriousness that was palpable. I felt that he already had one step in a different world, one that he could see but I could only dimly sense. When he said Mass, usually there were only the pair of us. However others participated that he was aware of, ethereal figures I only occasionally glimpsed, about whom we would later talk. Early each morning he disappeared down a nature trail for his morning meditation. He'd stroll into camp before breakfast, say almost nothing except for the simple greeting, "Pax" (Peace!). I always looked forward to the evening meditations, where he took us into a world that we never dreamed existed. He showed us the door and how to go through it.

Andrew was much in demand as a speaker on spirituality both in student and secular groups. His retreats given in Polish communities were always jammed full. In the mid-sixties he led regular courses for the Wrekin Trust at Attingham Park in Shropshire. Later he led seminars along with Sir George Trevelyan, the healer Bruce MacManaway and Sufi teacher Reshad Feild. His topics included human fields, music, gravitational waves, healing, meditation and our cooperation with the world of angels. Even those who didn't quite understand his scientific lexicon admitted that they felt a new zest for life following his talk. That Andrew had shown them a world that was much larger than the humdrum world of daily chores and routines. A world full of meaning.

Many legends circulated about him, that he could see and communicate with fairies, the spirits of druids, angels, perform miraculous healings. That he could not only heal over large distances, but was aware of events as they happened far away. Nobody doubted that he was a very spiritual person and that he moved in worlds that most others could not see. However as a man he remained an enigma.

In this book I have gathered transcripts of his talks and writings, hoping that they will find a wider audience. I am particularly indebted to John MacManaway who gave me several tapes of Andrew's talks given around 1969 in Scotland.

Many of Andrew's writings are technical and require of the reader some background in physics. Other talks in this volume, those on prayer, meditation and theology are more easily understood by the lay person. Common to both genres is the biological human field which he regarded as the unifying factor between spiritual and natural worlds. Rather than dividing the book into spiritual and scientific topics, I have chosen to interweave them, as he often did when presenting them. The first chapters lay the groundwork for future discussions by introducing the human field and exploring its spiritual role. Some chapters such as his discussions on the Holy Trinity and the Eucharist are largely theological. The science of the field and the process of healing through the field are explored in detail in Chapters 13 and 14, both reprints of Andrew's technical papers. Medical practitioners and those familiar with Reiki or Therapeutic Touch may find those chapters of particular interest.

I have conducted only minimal editing of the talks, changing words where necessary for clarity. Andrew spoke a "pigeon English" with a strong Polish accent, that overlooked the niceties of grammar. I wanted to preserve something of his unique accent, his ordering of words. Often in his choice of words and in his sentence structure, more comes across than the mere words. Something of his passion. In places I have abbreviated discussions to avoid too much repetition of material already presented.

Today I find his teaching is more relevant than ever. While his approach is undoubtedly Christian, it crosses all religious and dogmatic barriers and has been well-received by religious and agnostic alike. Young people were drawn to him. Following a workshop for young people held by the Wrekin Trust, the students were amazed to find out that Andrew was actually a Catholic priest, not a de-frocked priest but actually in charge of an active parish.

Andrew died the 6 November 1973 while at Hawkwood College where he was leading a workshop. For several years he had been suffering from angina. On the evening before his death he was walking with Doctor Gordon Barker down a corridor toward a meeting room to deliver a talk. Seeking relief from his angina he stopped by a potted rose in the hallway. He said to the rose, "Help me sweetie." After a few moments of standing close to the rose, he walked on, more easily. The next morning the rose had collapsed. His funeral at his parish church was attended by over a hundred people including fifty-six priests and three bishops. Ironically it was delayed because the undertakers couldn't get the lid to stay on the coffin.

1

THE SCIENCE
BEHIND HEALING[1]

The problem of healing can be approached from three different angles. The first is from physics and biophysics, a topic so large that to cover the ground I would need much more than ten to twelve lectures. A dissertation. The second is a psychological approach, which already has been done by Jung, the famous doctor and psychologist in Switzerland. The third is, strange enough, art. Perhaps I will have time to say a little about the artistic approach. Anyway, if there are any doctors here, they will know that medicine is an art.

My research started when I was a twelve year old boy. In those days I was thinking about atoms, and atomic physics. And strange enough in the town where I used to go to school, and my father used to work[2], there was a physicist, a scientist who produced ball lightning in his laboratory. It ran like mercury around the table. It made a terrific light. This phenomenon was the result of about fifty or sixty years of his researches. He invented Hertzian waves well before Hertz published his first paper on the subject, because it was around 1860, long before Maxwell even published his papers on electromagnetic waves. However he kept it in strict secret until the early 20th century, when my father, through a friend who was very close to the late engineer Alesnowski, that was the man, decided to found an institute and finance it. Eighteen doctors were employed. Alesnowski donated his peculiar machine. It was a sort of Wimshurst machine but differently constructed, to collect the par-electric energy. I call it par-electric as it was definitely not electric. He used it for healing purposes. The institute functioned for many years. No one was hurt. Practically everyone felt better after treatment. The doctors were very intrigued with the force field. That set me to think.

Not until I came to this country in 1940 when I encountered the first, really serious research into extra-sensory perception, did I start to conduct some methodical research into the subject. Before that I attended different universities throughout Europe, studied for nine years in my own town, different subjects, theology and science included. Throughout the continent in different universities, I collected data about human radiation, and possible explanations of the facts of this institute in the town where I had lived. When I came to this country I had a system, a sort of theosophical system or rational system. To my astonishment in 1946, just after the war, someone gave me a work written by an engineer, Louis Turenne, that had all the appearances of a scientific work, with graphs, mathematics, lots of figures although not proper mathematics as I saw. I started to study it; there were several volumes of this work, a dissertation on dowsing, but his arguments were absolutely insufficient.

I was sceptical about the whole business. Couldn't believe it. But still curiosity prevailed. I continued to collect data on the phenomena. Well eventually, I found myself having doubts. The divining rod was working in my hands like mad. Why? What's the matter with it? It works; there's no doubt about it. So I enrolled in the British Dowsing Society. I thought I would meet some people there who could explain the phenomena to me in terms of modern science. There was quite a lot of talking, quite a lot of experiments done but still no scientific explanation.

Later, around 1947 I found that I myself could heal. At a distance. That was too much for my poor brain: to understand how it's possible to diagnose and heal a person who is some miles, a hundred miles or a thousand miles away from me. It wasn't making sense to me at all. I was really puzzled by it but being a physicist I started to think what possible radiation was involved. Well I had been through all kinds of yoga studies, looked at Gurwitsch, Cazamalli, all sorts of Russian studies on this subject. When I was in Germany with the British occupation army, in 1946, a doctor brought me this work, "In Search of Bi-Quantas" by a Russian professor. Upon reading it I found out that in some Russian universities there were at least two chairs for the study of para-psychological phenomena. So obviously they wanted to study the subject properly.

There's no doubt that the phenomena are there. I've seen people being healed by hands. I've seen people being diagnosed at a distance, where the doctors have later investigated, and found that the diagnosis is dead right. How on earth was it done? I looked at the phenomena of yogis; also extra-sensory perception but I still couldn't make sense of it. Eventually when I myself learned to heal and find out how it is done, I saw that the phenomenon boils down to the field. To the human field.

Those who are trained in physics know about fields, but for those who aren't, I have to explain it. You sometimes talk about the field of knowledge, the field of research, meaning a domain of research. Now, a field in physics means a stress in a space around a certain object. Generally speaking, a stress. For example a certain tension in the air surrounding a human body. Now the research on the human field was started by Hans Spemann, a famous German biologist and embryologist in the early 1920s[3], later on picked up by Burr, Lane and Nims of Yale University[4], where the neurological and anatomical department conducted a tremendous amount of research on human fields. They produced special instruments, vacuum tubes, electrometers and very sensitive micro-voltmeters. The phenomenon of the human field is today known. But strange enough the researchers didn't think of some things that are quite obvious, that there is no need to propose some sort of phenomenal radiation. I was talking to a professor of physics in Cambridge who was interested in that sort of thing. He said to me, "Don't you postulate a new force?" I said, "I do but I don't have proof of it, but for ball lightning. I have done quite a lot of experiments. I can show a lot of things in the laboratory, such as the suspension of gravity, but it's not enough for my scientific and critical mind to prove such a force exists."

But there is a very simple phenomenon. We generate a field by emitting heat —infra-red radiation. What is infra-red radiation? For those who don't know, it's the same kind of radiation as light waves, or wireless waves—electromagnetic radiation. Every one of us emits infrared which later causes heat in the vicinity of the body. It travels with the speed of light, 186,000 miles per second. Now, what's important is not the strength of the field but its pattern, formed by the superposition of electromagnetic waves emitted by every cell in our body, by the surface of the skin. The pattern is unique to each one of us. In one eighth of a second this field covers the entire earthly globe, and, depending on your age, extends on into space for twenty or sixty light years—far into the galaxy, far into interstellar space. And if I were to go to the edge of my field and look back at the Earth, it would be like looking through a telescope, and there far away would be the Earth and my body. My field covers this colossal space. This field of heat contains my unique pattern.

If there are any medical people here, they would know that in medicine today we use the medical thermogram—a photograph of the skin in infra-red radiation. Strange to say this field shows a heat pattern of the skin that shows certain illnesses, certain dysfunctions.

This pattern changes with our moods, with the emotions of our personality. Today in medicine and in psychology there is a very well-known movement that started with Hans Selye, who devoted 20 or 30 years of his researches to the influence of emotions on human health. He published a paper called, "The study of adaptation syndrome" in 1951. Since then most universities have accepted this theory, because it's obvious that our emotions have a definite influence on our health pattern. Also, that over 80% of all illnesses are due to emotional stress. There's no doubt about it. Emotions change the pattern of our infra-red field.

Infra red waves have a wavelength of several microns[5]. Now those waves add up, one here, and another a little bit longer, and another still a bit longer, to build what we call in physics, a wave form. In three dimensions, this heat forms a pattern, a unique pattern that changes with the person's mood. This radiation carries with it the picture of its form. So in the radiation surrounding the human body, in the field, you have all information about the human body, everything that is going on in your metabolic exchange. In the future, medics will look into the field for that information and not into the body as they do now, because the field carries much more information: about you and your emotions, much more than you can find out through the chemistry of the body.

Another form of radiation that surrounds the human body is sound. A doctor working with a stethoscope uses sound to make a diagnosis. Just as when you're in a car, if you hear a *dic dic dic*, you know that there is something wrong with the machine. Back in the 17th century Robert Hooke, who was secretary of the Royal Society, of which Newton was president, wrote Newton a letter in which he said that in the future, the doctor instead of using a very crude instrument such as the stethoscope will use something much better for diagnosis, because the friction of the body's moving parts carries information on what is going on in the engine of the human body. The stethoscope is a crude instrument. Today you can measure the body's sound with a sensitive microphone, project the sound onto a cathode ray tube, which is like a television screen, see the wave form which sound produces and by analyzing the waveform get all sorts of information about dysfunctions in the human body. So that is a second field.

There is a third field, and that is electrical potential, evident when you take off your shirt and hear it crackle. Research on the electrical potential of the human body has been done for quite a long time. Sometimes it reaches 14,000 volts, but it's usually around 600-700 volts. Electrocardiograms and electro-cephalograms work on its basis. The change in the electric potential of the skin gives you information on what is going on inside.

This electrical potential influences your field. Somebody here may know something about the workings of a wireless, that when you hook up a diode valve, you connect it to the earth. The diode connected to the Earth is a very good condenser and this connection is the electric potential of the air. This is important, as you'll see later on, that when you sense the field with your hand, you are actually changing the field and by clearing the field, you are clearing the body. Why? Because there is a feedback phenomenon.

What is feedback? If you put an electrical signal, such as from a microphone, into an amplifier, you can take part of the emerging signal and put it back into the same amplifier. Now it's known in biology that every neurological cell and practically every biological cell works through feedback. So if you consider an organism as the sum of many cells where every biological cell also has a feedback, part of your energy goes out and part is fed back in. But when the energy that should return is refracted for some reason and doesn't return, you are lacking a certain pattern of radiation, and according to that pattern, a respective organ may be gradually affected.

Just as every radiation carries with it a picture of itself, like a photographic camera, so the radiation around the human body tells you in exact detail what is going on in the human body. In addition, this radiation is the function of your metabolic exchange, and through feedback it may bring you health or, if this feedback is lacking, you may deteriorate in due time.

This field is also related to the Psycho-Physical field, for the simple reason that its radiation will also change according to your mood. If you're angry, very angry, not only do your blood vessels change but within one minute your red blood corpuscles increase by one million. Your temperature rises, your capillary vessels enlarge. You're making all sorts of noises. What's happening? You're in a cramp. In the meantime your skin emits more energy because your capillary vessels enlarge and more heat is emitted. So obviously, the field around you is totally different because of your anger. If you are frightened, you become pale and your field emits much less heat. So, your moods, your emotions are reflected in the field. From your field you will not only find information on your metabolic exchange, but all information about your moods. About your temporary moods or permanent moods. And if you are jealous, it will definitely affect your field, your electromagnetic field in the form of infra-red radiation. Your sonic field will be affected as well. I have shown elsewhere in a paper, The Gravitational Wave[6] so I won't present details here, how sound affects the electrostatic field. Your electrostatic field will be affected as well, and your feedback loop. So as a result of jealously, certain organs, the liver in particular, will be deprived of their feedback—the energy coming back to you. After a while you'll feel that your liver is suffering. Anyway, they say that jealous people are yellow, and there may be something in it.

I come to certain practical results I got through my hands. When you move your hands around the body, or someone else's body you can feel, at certain distances, a faint sensation: maybe prickling or a certain heaviness, coolness or heat. At certain distances the heat is quite distinct. If you have a very sensitive thermometer, you'll find that the temperature increases to a certain point, then decreases, increases and so on. Exactly like what is going on above the Earth where the temperature decreases up to twenty miles above the surface and then increases and goes through cycles. Because infra-red radiation waves superimposed on one another make a certain interference pattern. The body's field seen from a bird's eye view has certain layers that can be felt by the hand. If you introduce your own field into somebody else's field, tune in with the use of the imagination to investigate this field, the electrical nervous impulses will pass through the hands and so to your nervous system, and you will feel only what you want to find out. It's your moods that produce your sensitivity to this peculiar field. And I found to my amazement that these layers around the human body are not regularly spaced, but form a pattern, a cluster here, then nothing, then another cluster.

Those of you who know some atomic physics will know what I'm talking about when I talk about eigen-values. The nucleus of an atom is a harmonic oscillator. Now the human body is a harmonic oscillator too, simply because the metabolic exchange is still in motion, in vibration. It boils down eventually to atoms. If you do the summation of 1 to n, if every atom is a harmonic oscillator then the sum must be a harmonic oscillator too. It's a simple mathematical problem. You can do the Fourier Analysis if you want to. Now, these eigenvalues around the human body do exist and you can feel them. And not only me, or Major MacManaway or someone who claims, "I'm a healer." Every one of you can do exactly the same, just as every one of you can learn to read or write, or learn to play the piano. In exactly the same way, everyone can learn to cure the field. You may find out, for instance, in sensing the spectrum of the human field, a certain dysfunction, two or three peaks that are strong. You put your hand there, never mind how to do it, and with your hand you can clear that pattern. And that particular pattern of heat and sound will not be refracted, but will be reflected back to the human being, so that the feedback is re-introduced. And once the feedback is restored, the subject will feel much better.

I find the bio-chemical approach too crude. Generally I approach the human being as a very complicated electrical network. Every nerve is carrying an electrical current, every biological cell produces electrical activity in its electrolytes. Medical students here know that pH and rH are electrical quantities. It's all a big electrical factory, and this electrical factory must have an electrical field around itself. If you start to work with this field, you are much closer to the actual structure of the illness than you can be with chemistry. With chemistry you can find out something but if a certain pattern is lacking in the field, it may not show up in the chemistry.

I've explained in a very general way, how the technical side of the human field works. It remains to say a few words about the psychological aspect of this problem, and how this whole thing links with faith. Suppose that one of you whom I just met has an intense dislike for me. Fair enough, I don't blame you. And we meet at various social gatherings. Eventually my friends tell me, "This Bill hates you." Well, I'll not pay attention to the first friend, but then the next one tells me and then the next and finally I start to believe it. And once I start to believe, instead of going to Bill and saying to him, "Do you really hate me or not?" I believe it and become resentful, develop a negative emotion, and this negative emotion penetrates my nervous system, and from there enters the field. Through this set of beliefs, and this is a belief, that he hates me, I stir up certain negative emotions, that in turn create a nervous tension in me, and this in turn stirs up a negative functioning in part of my body, fitting with my emotional pattern, and my emotional distress. So you can see that belief can be a very important factor in stirring up emotions and producing a real dysfunction in the body. But it can also be a revitalizing process. If I for instance harbour hatred through a set of beliefs that Bill doesn't like me, that he wants to kill me, but after a certain time I realize that he is my friend, the emotion will dissolve. What a relief! Immediately the correct electrical signals are sent through my nervous system, all the nervous tension is released and out of the blue I'm back to normal again. Anger, lust, they will affect my kidneys. Shaking that, I am normal again. And there's no use in taking pills when the root of the cause is psychological. A set of beliefs. So you can see that a set of beliefs has definitely a bearing on the problem of health.

If Christ said, "Your faith has saved you," he referred to the set of beliefs that somebody can release my cramp right here, my negative attitude toward life. When Christ healed, he always did something, he moved his hands, or he did something. And this something had an effect. He said that a set of beliefs opens the gate to something that saves you.

Perhaps there are university students here. You believe that you can cope with the difficulty of a course at the university. If you believe that you can be an engineer, and architect or say a doctor, this belief opens for you the gate. It doesn't give you the knowledge but it opens the way so you dare to go and start to study. Nothing else. So this set of beliefs is the opening of the gate but it's not the whole thing. So when we refer to "faith healing" it's not the faith as such. Faith opens the gate; relaxes your negative tensions, brings you to peace with yourself. And that may be the basis for further improvement in your health, but there must be action from another plane.

I'm a theologian. I studied theology since 1923. For nine years I was a student at various universities throughout the continent. And when I finished, I still think that I just started A and B, but hadn't done C. But I knew that when Christ laid-on hands and cured, it was nothing to do with some sort of miraculous business, because Grace never destroys nature but builds upon nature. And further, it enhances natural phenomena, brings strength to natural phenomena but never contradicts nature. And therefore, there must be a natural law behind this healing phenomenon. There's no doubt about it. And this theological argument doesn't destroy faith whatsoever. It reinforces it. Because faith is a rational business. Not irrational, something out of the blue. God has given you and me and all the others a reasoning ability, so all our beliefs must be reasonable things. I knew that if I looked for the science behind healing, something would come up in the natural world. Something did, and that was the Field Theory. The force field is what I call the Psycho-Physical field. That means, my psychological phenomena, my psychological moods, my psychological collapse or elations will be reflected in the field, and will, clear the field or make it denser according to my positive or negative emotions.

A new development recently occurred. Last week, Stanley Backster showed on the TV program "Tomorrow's World" how plants a thousand miles will respond immediately with an electrical response, detected with an amplifier attached to a graph pen, to any trouble of the owner or gardener a thousand miles away.[7] How is that possible? And how is it possible that I can diagnose at a distance and cure people? If my field covers the Earth in one eighth of a second, obviously my field is everywhere, just as wireless waves are everywhere. If you tune in, like fine tuning a wireless, you can hear it. You may say, "My field is very weak". Very well, but you are not tuning into a single wavelength but into a certain pattern, and this pattern makes detection possible.[8] I won't go into the technical side, only to say that if the field is everywhere, if I tune in I do not tune into the field at a distance. I tune into the field here, wherever you are. It doesn't matter.

You may have read, *An Experiment in Time* by John Dunne. Sometimes when you are dreaming, you see some events. Then two days later those events happen to you. Time is a field as well. Or you go to a place where you've never been that feels familiar, and then you find out that you dreamed of it. How did you find that place in your dream? With your eyes? Your eyes were closed in bed. How did you see those different things? By your field. Your field picks up signals from far away and brings them back to you. Infra red radiation goes out into the surroundings, reflects and brings back information, in impulses that are so weak that they are below the threshold of consciousness. You don't notice them. But if in a dream, you remove the blockages, the threshold of consciousness goes down, then a very weak impulse can reach your consciousness. You can see in dream a place that later on you come upon, and think that you've been there before. Well, simply you were there. Let me tell you that this exploration of the Moon is an old fashioned thing. Sorry to disappoint you, but your field has been there since your childhood. One and a half seconds is the time for your infra-red radiation to travel to the Moon, and to bring you information from there, but you have been blocking yourself in every way so as not to receive that signal from outside.

There's another thing that you'll laugh at to begin with. Do you know where your thinking is going on? It's in your field. You'll say, "That's rubbish." I'll give you an example. Let's go 200 years back in time to 1768, and bring a wireless with you. You'll say to people, "This is a wireless, and it plays." They say, "Who is talking there?" You tell them, "That's only a box. The talking is in the air." They'll say, "What? The talking is in here." You tell them, "This is only a transformer that brings you the sound." "I beg your pardon. Don't pull my leg. That's not true because I hear the box thing talking. It's not in the air. I can't feel anything there. That's nonsense."

Well, it's exactly the same when I tell you that your head is not thinking. That the thinking is in your field—the Organizing Field, so nicely described by Gustaf Stromberg, and in experiments I mentioned.[9] [10] Your thinking is in your field; the brain is your transformer, the wireless that brings it to your consciousness. As I told you, if you go to the perimeter of your field, somewhere twenty light years distant, and look back with a telescope, you'll see the Earth far away, and somewhere in it, your body. But you have done everything throughout your life to limit yourself to your body. That is not me. That is my transformer of consciousness to the physical field. If you study Stromberg's paper on the Organising Field, you'll find out that it is outside space and time. I don't have time to go into that, but it is a non-physical field, a Primary Field. Stromberg calls it the Soul. He says that's the only way he can talk about it but the name doesn't matter. It's something that is outside space and time. I have been talking to you today about the Secondary Field transmitted by your body. However the Organizing Field is the cause of it. It influences your body. Your thinking takes place through the Organizing Field, which is outside space and time, and therefore the whole universe is affected by it. This theory of fields can explain many phenomena: telepathy, how plants respond to your moods, your thoughts and your anger; many extra-sensory phenomena are immediately explained, there where a solution should be found. So also the healing.

Someone came to me and said, "Father." (I don't like to be called, *Father*. I usually call myself *Andrew*. This *Father* stuff is all corrupt and puts walls between ourselves. We have to be really one family and love one another.) So he says, "Andrew, something is wrong with my eyes. Could you do something?" It was a youngster I knew who had trouble with his sight. I knew that there is probably a pressure somewhere on the glandular system here. So, I start to clear the field with my hand. To my astonishment, all his hair stands up like this. Then his hair started to follow my hand. Obviously an electrical phenomenon was involved.

I don't want to go into technicalities of why it happened. It just did. Many people write to me and say, I'm ill or this or that; could you do something about it? And as their writing is a sample of their personality, because it has the same set of proportions, then I can use it to tune into their field. Their field that is present here, is reinforced by the writing or a piece of hair; sort of amplified. Again, don't ask me why, but it's a reasonable explanation. And that's how I can introduce myself into your field. I'm not healing at a distance, but I'm beside you because your field is here. Now present.

Now a bit on the artistic side. If you look at my face and that of Major MacManaway, you recognize that is Major MacManaway and here is Andrew who talks and talks too long. And by what do you recognize it? By a set of proportions; the set of proportions of my face. You distinguish the set of proportions of my face from this table. It has its set of proportions. And actually what you observe visually—a set of proportions, or by hearing; it's also a set of proportions, like the quality of the voice or of a musical instrument. We are dealing always with a set of proportions.

A crystal has a set of proportions, a beautiful architectural structure. There was a German scientist called Gottlieb, a famous scientist who investigated the set of proportions of a crystal and the angles of reflection, and he found out that these proportions are, strangely enough, a musical set of proportions. And another German scientist, Doctor Mayer Ibach began to investigate crystals. Actually he was from Hamburg University. He came to me when I was there in 1947[11], and we spent five hours talking. He knew I was interested in this subject. At the time he was writing the history of medicine. He said something that impressed me, that, in medicine, we would only obtain accurate knowledge when we introduced mathematics into it. How on Earth could we introduce mathematics into medicine? Now I know, because if you prove that the human body is a result of electrical phenomena and electrical networks, then it's obvious. You can get to the diagnosis by measuring differences in the electric field.

He called my attention to the book by Hans Kayser, *Harmonia Plantarum*. I brought part of this book here. After studying crystals, Kayser started to measure the set of proportions of plants. He found that they worked out as 3,4,17,10 and so on. It eventually boils down to music.

Because in music, if you take the middle C on the piano, 256 vibrations per second and a certain length of the string, a certain tension and so on, then the next harmonic, an octave higher, will have a string of half of this length but will vibrate twice as much, 512 vibrations per second. The next harmonic will vibrate three times as much, and the length will be a third, then the fourth. So he took middle C as unity, and he wrote the harmonics as 1/1, 2/1, 3/1, 4/1. The major scale set of proportions. Going down from C he found the minor scale set of proportions. And applying this to plants he found that plants grow above the ground in a major scale set of proportions and below the ground in a minor scale set of proportions. And he wrote a book about that. Fascinating book. Then he applied the knowledge of harmonics to the whole of human life, and that's this book, *Lehrbuk der Harmonik*.[12] First there's the scientific, mathematical treatment and then the art. The artwork shows how the human body functions as a harmonic oscillator as well. It's harmonically built, an art form in itself (Figure 1). If you go into the physics, you find that the atom is a harmonic oscillator reverberating to the main field in the nucleus, and that is the music of the atom. So obviously the human body is a collection of oscillations, of music and artwork in itself. So you can see the artistic side of this.

This is why in a certain Paris hospital they'll prescribe for you to listen three times a day to the sound of a raindrop, or the D major sonata of Beethoven because there are certain tones there, and there are certain tones in the dysfunctional sonic field that must be abolished. Now that can again be very painstakingly analyzed by computers, to find out what tones are for what illness, and how art or music can penetrate the human field and affect your health.

I have been talking to you, only touching on, giving you a glimpse of a possible scientific approach of why you can heal with your hands. You heal the field. You restore the feedback, and through that feedback the body starts to recover. It's not that you heal the body. You heal the radiation and reintroduce feedback into the body. There is no doubt about it, that that is the future of the medical profession. I call it Psycho-Physical Field Therapy. It can be computerized, but I don't think that any computer will cope with it. As Graywater said, if you want to make a computer like the human head, the whole United Kingdom would not have enough space to contain all the electrifiers required to calculate all the possibilities of minute quantities, minute volumes.

Imagine only that you have to hit a tennis ball. How many computations do you have to make in a fraction of a second: where the ball

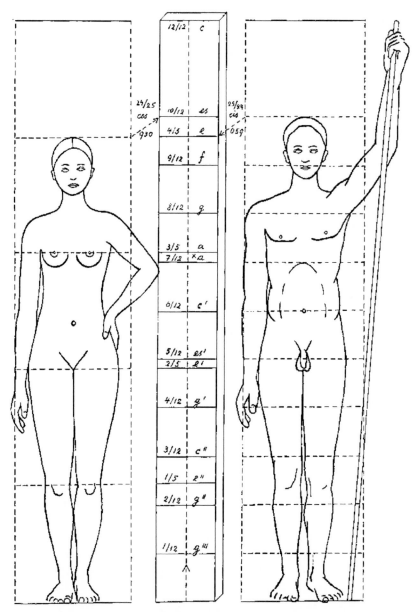

Figure 1: The Harmonic Proportions of the Human Body,
from "Lehrbuk der Harmonik" by Hans Kayser.

goes, what direction, what sort of wind, how you have to place yourself to hit the ball, what sort of speed to use and where you have to put
the ball. That's the computations you have to make in a fraction of a
second. If you want a book on that, try *Psychocybernetics*[13]. A doctor
wrote it, all about psychological computation. Fascinating book. Pure
science; very little mathematics. It's the only book around that tells
you about the power of your imagination. It's not the power of your
will. It's your imagination that brings you the possibilities in your life.
If you see yourself an engineer, you will be an engineer. In every faith
or set of beliefs, you have to picture yourself as that or that.

There is no accident in your life. Accidents happen because of yourself, your own disorientation in your subconscious mind. I would have
to go into the analysis of your subconscious, conscious, and the overconscious. The overconscious I call the High Self. It's the life of God in
us if you want. It doesn't matter what you call it. It's still tremendous
knowledge and tremendous love. And then from that point of view if you
start to produce a real prayer based on modern psychology, meditation,
this meditation introduces you at once to the life of the subconscious
and overconscious mind. You don't need a drug for that. You develop
your subconscious mind with a little work and you start to develop
your extra-sensory perception. Educated people, with a high standard
of education use only one millionth of a millionth of their brain, and
the rest is latent. Just fast asleep. When you see this then you may realize how powerful Man can be. What a giant he is. How his thinking
is going on in his field, and how the Earth is only a spec. And that is
only one level. We can go into different frequencies of time and then
you see a totally different world. The Ideas of Plato.

Anyway I wanted to give you a sort of glimpse of the future of medicine. Field medicine. There's no doubt also that you yourself can heal.
Every one of you can help yourself, help your family. All the children
of my parish have been taught. And when the mums and dads have
headaches, or other ailments, they're treated before they go to the doctor. They relieve the doctors a tremendous lot. This does not by any
means abolish the chemical method. It is very important. The doctors
do their utmost to cure people, but they haven't got the physical application. Physics is essential, and psychology as well. Put yourself in
the world of proportions, musical proportions. Never mind if it's of astronomical size; Kepler showed in *Harmonices Mundi*, that heavenly
bodies are moving according to harmonic laws, a set of proportions.
Or you go into the set of proportions of the world of the atom, or of

everyday life. It's always the same set of proportions. And once you go deeply into that world, then space doesn't exist. You meet that set of proportions everywhere, and you can move according to the possibilities of your wave pattern.

Well this is how I started thinking about the interpretation of how the hand can produce feedback in terms of sound, electromagnetic radiation, heat, Psycho-Physical, or electrostatic fields. The interpretation may be entirely different. I have been experimenting most of my life, but now my hands are tied. I haven't got the money nor the possibilities or the laboratory for further experiments.

But I am quite sure of these three things. That everybody can cure, that there is a field medicine, and that you can go into quite a different world when you start to live in the world of proportions, when you meet the world of the subconscious and overconscious mind. And that is more or less what I can tell you in an hour and a half. An outlook of what is to be if you analyze the healing hand.

2

ANGELS[1]

To begin with, angels are not winged creatures with nice faces. They are certain patterns of proportions; intellectual patterns that are self-conscious as we are self-conscious. Just that we have a body, neck and head and they haven't got them.

Now what I mean by a set of proportions is something which we have to investigate from different angles. If I see you and see somebody else, I recognize you from the set of proportions of your face. I distinguish a table from a chair by its set of proportions. So we have to realize that we are constantly moving among sets of proportions as such, and those sets of proportions are perceptible, and when we connect them, then we form a picture of a man or an object or a sensation. So the sets of proportions surround our perceptions.

Now angels are something of a set of proportions in that sense but without being incarnate or having a body. If you take the personality as such, the personality is itself a set of proportions. Actually in theology, we know that the virtue of prudence, for example, is what brings a set of proportions into balance: the balancing factor in the character of a person that tells you, not too much or too little. Just the right proportions. Now this is my hand, a good hand that has a certain natural set of proportions.

Once we have established what we mean by a set of proportions, we have to establish further that what we call our set of proportions is reflected in our field. Your field is the result of your physical, emotional and mental life. It is also a set of proportions that according to the way you think and imagine things, sends respective impulses throughout your body corresponding to your emotions, every minute, that produce a change in your field. So your set of proportions reflects your moods.

Your field is something that is outside your body, as a set of proportions, and which is actually related to electromagnetic phenomena as well as other mechanical phenomena such as sound. But when I talk about an angel as a set of proportions that is aware of itself, I'm talking about a different thing. Once you realize that your thinking is in the field and not in your brain, the brain only being a transformer from the inner field set of proportions to the material field, then you will realize what an angel is. You can call it a set of proportions in a field, which is not the Secondary Field arising from electromagnetic and other phenomena, but is the Primary Field which we call, Soul[2]. But if you want to expand on this conception of Soul then the angel would be the Primary Field without manifestation in the material world. But I suppose it can create a manifestation in the physical field, such as electromagnetic and so on, by the power of his will. Of his consciousness. This, an angel who is your partner for life, is somebody who has a similar set of proportions as you and therefore he is in relationship with you. And we call it our Angel Guardian—the name is irrelevant. It is your partner. It is somebody who fits with your set of proportions, and therefore he is connected with you. As your set of proportions are outside space and time, therefore your angel is outside space and time. It doesn't matter if you are here or you are there. This set of proportions is with you everywhere. Just as the set of proportions 3,4,7,8 and so on, is not necessarily bound by space or with time. It's outside all those phenomena. Now that is an angel. Its set of proportions can be compared to a kaleidoscope, to pictures you observe in a kaleidoscope. You have to imagine them not in two dimensions but in three dimensional space, although they're made of glass pieces. Because the set of proportions produces a certain kind of presence in space, therefore he can express certain properties of light that I can see, an optical set of proportions, so beautiful that you are absolutely held by it. You can't take your eyes off it.

MacManaway: And you can't describe it.

AG: It's impossible to describe it. How can I describe it? It's a personality by itself. An angel. According to theologians, every angel is a species unto itself, because it exists in its specific strata. Each one is absolutely unique, as is each human being. As is every atom.

18

MacManaway: Even every atom?

AG: Yes. It's a pattern by itself. There are human sets of properties, plant sets of proportions. According to the work of Hans Kayser, *Die Harmonik*, they're all harmonic phenomena. If you take middle "C" on the piano, 256 cycles per second, then the next octave is twice that, 512, the next is 1024 octave and so forth. The first one is represented in standard notation as 1/1, the second will be 2/1, 4/1. If you go downward from middle "C" you have ½, 1/3, ¼ so on. So once you get into the world of proportions as such, which are always musical proportions, also in the field, then you go into the place where 3/4 or 7/8 is irrespective of space. Therefore it doesn't matter whether an angel is of atomic size or astronomical size. It is still 7/4 and therefore every atom and every astronomical body will have its own partner, according to the set of proportions of the field. And that agrees with statements of old theologians as Thomas Aquinas who concluded that every planet has its own angel. Its own partner. But, concluding from our investigation, every atom would have its own partner as well, because it is a set of proportions. How can an atom have a partner for an angel, or a planet? We know from the Bible that every region, every glen has its own angel, but how on Earth can every atom?

We don't understand it because we still have the concept of size in our mind. But in the world of proportions there is no size. The funny thing is that though we actually move in the world of proportions, we constantly refer to ourselves in terms of our size and not as a set of proportions. Here is the real difference between the spiritual and physical worlds. But we have to remove the concept of size, and then we find ourselves in a totally different world, on a different level, but still in the world of proportions.

From this you can understand what angels are. A few words about the different levels. The Scriptures tell us about nine choirs. Well, maybe they've explored the whole thing. Maybe there are nine, maybe an infinite number. I don't know. I haven't got a clue. But the fact is that those levels are so distinct from one another that, according to Thomas Aquinas[3], a lower angel cannot talk to a much higher angel, unless he uses certain channels, because he speaks a different language. He has a specific set of proportions that will not communicate with that of angels very high up. So he has to go through the usual channels, from one choir to another, and then a higher angel will understand what he is talking about. If I talk German to you, which you can't understand, I can't communicate with you because the language has a different set of proportions from English. But in the angelic world you have a different phenomenon which is called Grace, or participation in divinity, and this is participation in divine life. In view of the enlightened divine set of proportions which are unique for some, those angels can communicate immediately between all levels. So here you have the species of angels. If you talk using a long-wave radio set you can't tune into it with a short-wave radio. But if you have a converter, then you can. The same thing occurs between angels.

The lower angels are much more complicated than the higher ones. The higher you go the simpler they are. Theologians say that God conceived the whole world through one word, one concept and that means his own Son. The higher angels must have at least two concepts. We have immense concepts for each particular object. But always, a set of proportions enters our mind. The mind attempts to adjust its set of proportions to the object, and then they match, and we understand. Angels are sets of proportions harmonically, harmonics but of different kinds. Here we have an explanation for the choir.

The third thing that is essential about angels is that they are serving spirits, as St. Paul says in his letter to the Hebrews. What does this mean? It's that their essence is to serve, not to be served. It's expressed in the Bible where St. Michael said, or Our Lady said, "Lord let it be according to thy will." They are obedient. Now what does obedience mean? It doesn't mean that I give you orders and you carry them out. You are listening to the laws of nature, and then when you listen properly to them and grasp them, then according to the laws of nature the angel will obey you.

MacManaway: Through resonance?

AG: Yes. Obedience means a resonance; fitting into a certain pattern. In order to cooperate, a serving spirit needs a willingness to cooperate with somebody else, and not only with somebody else but with the whole universe. Because it grasps the harmony of the universe as something that fits in with them, which will enlarge their consciousness and will give them an infinite possibility of joy. Then the whole universe is playing with them, and they are playing with the whole universe. That is a serving spirit. The spirit that says, "I shall not serve" says, "I want the universe to fit in with me but I shall not fit in with the universe. Therefore I am miserable by myself." And that is the principle of those who have revolted.

So here you have the explanation of the serving spirits. They are willing to cooperate and willing to do anything they can to play the game with those they are connected to. The lower choirs are the Guardians, those who are specifically related to a certain object. The next choir is Archangels, then Principalities and so on until the Seraphim who are glowing spirits of love. They will not interfere with your pattern, they will let you play your music, but if you tell them to do something about your music because you are not yet very good, not yet the master of the instrument which you have to play, then they will do everything possible to help you. As a matter of fact they will always obey, and you can't give them a better pleasure than to tell them what you are fond of, because then they will mend your thinking, teach you to master your instrument so that they can enjoy the harmony coming from you. It is in their interest to do whatever they can for you, but they will respect your individuality and they will not interfere unless you tell them.

As every angel has its own particular pattern, every angel has a different function. One angel may be the angel of your home, but there are angels for each of your atoms, each of your organs which coalesce in the whole. You have millions of angels to yourself, to your body. You have another set of proportions which is your mental personality, your different needs and different moods, specific patterns for your joy, serenity, one for your anger and your desire. So in each case there is a different angel who is in charge of these things; specialists, for these are specialists. You can speak in any choir you want to but they can't. They are fixed in one pattern and they can't develop into another. But you can.

MacManaway: That's an interesting thought. They can't switch?

AG: No, they are fixed, because they haven't got a lever to change.[4] You can switch from the body to the field, from the field to the body. You are not a closed system while they are. So you can absorb two choirs, three choirs, any number of choirs and you can fit into all of them. You have that entire possibility in you while they don't. All of Creation, the entire being of the universe must be for Man, for he has all the possibilities; but all other creatures have nothing.

MacManaway: Can man help the angels climb the scale?

AG: No, because they are fixed by nature, by the set of proportions they have, in the fields that are ordained for them, though with tremendous possibilities. You have a cable; you can play anything on that cable but you can't go from a cable to a guitar, because the cable doesn't have a guitar socket. You have all the instruments of the orchestra within you, so you can go anywhere you want. That is the greatness, the potential greatness of human beings. You have strings that can play Brahms or percussion, can play anything you want. Tremendous possibilities.

It's fantastic how the human being is so great, with wings, and how far he can go with the help of those sets of proportions.

You have to tell the angels what you want and then they do it. I've told you how angels helped me in different ways. So unexpectedly. I'm amazed at how they care about my tastes. Somebody once prepared for me something I don't like and then forgot about it. She didn't give it to me. And then she wrote to me that she left it at the delicatessen. She forgot it because the angel didn't want her to send it to me, because I can't stand it. It's amazing how it works. I never have a parking problem, if I think of it in advance.

Remember always to thank them. Someone suggested very rightly that you thank them in advance, and then you have no problem when you receive something, but usually you're so thrilled by what you got that you forget to thank them. Well, you'd better thank them afterwards too, as you need to educate your spirit of thankfulness, which is extremely important for the development of your personality. Thankfulness opens you up to certain possibilities, and the angels can infuse a higher power in you when you are thankful. I can't yet properly grasp this, but they said that I would grasp it later on. Well, fair enough.

Often I discover that they do what is best for me. So I'm never discouraged if something that I want doesn't crop up because I know that they are doing the proper thing. The whole thing will crop up in the best possible way.

Once you have developed a sense of proportion, of proportionality, rather I should say a sensitivity to it, a clairvoyance to it, and you live in the world of proportions, then you contact them immediately, because proportions are proportions. But when you are steeped in material things, you don't conceive of what you can see in the field world. You may find a set of proportions that is beautiful. Why? Because it is beautiful. The flower is beautiful. Why? Well, I don't know, it's just beautiful. Eventually you see that it is beautiful in its fragrance, shape, the colour, the whole thing and all in its environment because the flower grows according to the field impinging on the flower, and it will be beautiful in its respective surroundings. Now if you abstract the material field from the shape and you go into the set of proportions, and you start to look, then you have contacted the angelic world. You start to perceive it, not with the human eye because you can't see the shape, but you can see the set of proportions.

MacManaway: One of the questions I know is going to crop up, something about which we have partial teaching, is the stream of evolution within which the angelic forces move. For example last weekend we had a conference on Pan, and the nature spirits. Into what relationship would Pan and the nature spirits, and the angelic hierarchy as you just described it relate? Is it one and the same stream? Are Pan and his nature spirits all part of the same set of proportions, one angelic stream?

AG: I think that there is only one set of proportions throughout the universe, throughout Creation. And as you have solid, liquid, gas, and further states, there must be further development. It's only the materialist scientist that says I can't touch it or I don't smell it and so it doesn't exist. It's absurd, because you can't touch a set of proportions or musical notes, or a musical theme, and what he actually experiences is this; a set of proportions, but he doesn't see it. Materialistic people are absolutely hopeless. They can't see what actually they are dealing with.

MacManaway: Now Andrew, in your vision, can there be any interchange between angelic beings and human beings?

AG: Constant. There are many instances that survive. There is an old tale of an angel who came to Palestine and said all sorts of things. We don't know. How many angels do we perceive on the street, maybe an infinite number of angels? They can assume the shape of a plant, or an animal. I haven't got a clue. Here I can't give you an answer; it's a totally different world. But I'm quite sure that they can in certain environments, and for a certain necessity, being serving spirits, assume different shapes, and appear to the human eye. To material eyes. What would this mean? They could condense air in such a way that they would reflect or refract light. And therefore they would condense the field so you would perceive them with the physical eye. If you need touch, they would condense the field further, because they are obviously very powerful in manipulating energy. Matter is nothing but a form of condensed energy. Or say, condensed lines of space in a certain set of proportions, or arranged in a certain pattern. I suppose that they can do that too. As we also can by the power of thought.

I would like to speak a little more about spirits; the nature of nature spirits. I told you about a scientist in this country who performed experiments with a revolving arm. It was an arm about two and a half yards long and it could revolve three hundred and sixty degrees. In the centre was a container with radioactive material, and at the end was an electrode connected to an amplifier and loudspeaker. Now when he put an element into the container, then the radioactive discharge moved the arm. Relative to the Earth's magnetic field the discharge was always at a certain angle depending on the element. He studied an entire sequence of elements from hydrogen to the higher elements, up to uranium, and then the lower Lanthanides, progressing higher and higher to the human being. Each of these elements has its own angle of discharge, where the discharge is most pronounced. But there remained ninety degrees free – left over. And he asked me, "What's there?" I said, "I don't know but probably higher beings than us." They might discharge there, but we can't put anything in the container. Well, it would be an interesting test. Would there be a discharge at that angle? If so then we'll know that it is related to nature spirits whatever they are. Or rather an appearance of nature spirits, spirits with a different set of proportions, but our eye doesn't pick them up because light doesn't reflect from them. Therefore we don't see them. Maybe they can bend light. It's quite easy to conceive of an instrument that could put a field around you that will bend light around you, therefore you would be invisible. I've seen photographs that seem to show them but I don't know.[5] I'm not saying 'no' and I'm not saying 'yes'. I'm just keeping an open mind. So that's what I can say about nature spirits. They may be a higher development or a lower development than us. They don't seem to be angelic beings. They're some sort of different creature. They're in resonance with the proportions of plants and with stones, and humans, but their nature is not so high. Not so spiritual. They may only be electromagnetic in nature, while angels are much higher than electromagnetic. If they are only electromagnetic, they should be detected by instruments we have now. Or they could have a special waveform, and because we haven't produced an instrument to detect such a wave form, we can't pick them up. Today the police use not a very high frequency band of superposed wavelengths for communication. Maybe one day someone will produce an instrument that picks up a waveform that will show all sorts of things in a room that we don't perceive. So that is one possible explanation for nature spirits that belong in a different world. I keep an open mind, because if people see something through the ages, independently, there must be something objective. So you have to keep an open mind.

3

THE MECHANICS OF
PRAYER[1]

I'm going to talk to you today about the Mechanics of Prayer. I'm not intending to talk about prayer as such from the conventional point of view because we have heard about it so many times and we have so many books, that this subject is well known to us. I intend to talk to you from a different angle, mostly from my own researches about prayer and its mechanical side. How it works.

There are two different and distinct elements in prayer, a natural and supernatural element. By supernatural I mean the element of Godhood as such, an uncreated being. We are all created with the angels, together. And whatever happens in us is only a manifestation of God's power. God Himself as an uncreated being is above all nature, and we, through Grace can participate in this tremendous privilege of being created; existing by adoption. To start with I would like to talk about the natural side of prayer. Why do we pray? The basis of our prayer is actually in our nature. We feel our insufficiency. We can't do everything we want and therefore we are seeking for a higher power to complement us. To support us. To give us power.

Now this insufficiency is two-fold, a spiritual side: insufficiency of knowledge, and insufficiency of love, will, or any sort of love coming from desire, emotional or spiritual. There is also an insufficiency from the point of view of our physical body. We can be killed, we are subject to death, to illness, to all sorts of suffering. That makes us, persons made out of body and soul, or body, mind and spirit, look for something much higher and much bigger.

Why higher? Strange enough, if you analyze prayer, we always speak about a higher power. Listen to the BBC program, "Lift up your hearts". Why up? Christ went up to the mountains to pray. Why? When he was crucified he said, "I must be elevated." You see there is a vertical component in prayer. This vertical component gives us food for thought. What are we looking for? Why is there an element of low—going down, and of high—going up? And usually—I haven't seen anybody who when he tends to pray, is going down. He's lifting his eyes. Now this element of higher has a spiritual element that has a physical basis. Strange enough the physical basis is gravity. Here I'm tackling the physical side of it.

Gravity is one of my subjects on which I wrote several papers. What is gravity? When you understand the nature of gravity, you will see the link between the phenomenon of gravity and prayer. What Newton said about the attraction of the bodies is only a sort of saying, because we know that a body doesn't have a mystical property to attract anything. Gravity is due to inertia, to mass in motion. "Momentum" we call it in physics. We can call it a curvature of space. After the Hungarian physicist Eotvos proved by experiment that inertial and gravitational phenomena are at least very much like one another, Einstein proved that actually inertia and gravity are identical phenomena. And that is the basis for Einstein's theory of gravity.

Now what is inertia? It's the power to resist a change of motion. Any change of motion or any acceleration must be produced by overcoming the inertia of matter, and that means gravity. Now we have in physics two kinds of inertia, physical inertia and electrical inertia which is called impedance. Impedance behaves a little like gravity but it's not exactly gravity. It's not exactly resistance but it behaves completely like resistance. Some would say a sort of spiritual resistance.

Now imagine first of all what would happen if we cut off gravity. You've heard about weightlessness in space. First of all the phenomenon of levitation is understandable. And here we have prayer. You may recall a story about St. Teresa. She was once praying in her cell when one of the nuns knocked at the door. "Come in." Strange enough the nun heard the voice from somewhere high. She saw St. Teresa bumping into the ceiling. She couldn't get down. Now if you take a very sensitive scale and stand on it, kneel or whatever, and you start to concentrate your mind on the subject of prayer, the needle will show you a loss of weight. The best experiment is to imagine yourself in Australia. I don't know if there are any Australians here, but if you imagine yourself to be on the opposite side of the globe, down there, and falling into space then immediately the needle on the scales will show you a difference, and the difference in your weight will be the measurement of your power of your concentration.

So you see, in prayer we are starting to lift ourselves up, overcome the force of gravity. Where does it lead to? To overcoming any sort of resistance. What does overcoming inertia mean? There are two inertias, the actual inertia of the body and the so-called imaginary inertia, spiritual inertia. We are all aware that we have spiritual inertia in ourselves and we know how much we have to fight to overcome it. Now if you suspend that, what will happen? No heavy work. No resistance. I can push the table, not only with my hand but with my thought. At first it produces a pressure so faint that it is hardly noticeable. If you overcome spiritual inertia, it won't be very hard, by choosing the path of least resistance, to be really good. Everybody wants to be good, but we have to overcome our spiritual inertia. If we can overcome that, then we are free.

I don't know if you've ever had an experience of getting out of your body. I have. And you can see your body lying there. What a freedom. No inertia. You just move. As an absolutely free butterfly you leave your cocoon which is an awfully heavy weight, a burden, and you are free. Wherever you think, there you are. And we know that after death, we are there where we think.

Anyway you can see how gravity and prayer are linked together. The vertical component tells you that you can free yourself from gravity or inertia or resistance, physical and spiritual, by your prayer; by lifting up yourself and be free. Enjoy freedom. What happens inside of us while we are lifting up ourselves or overcoming gravity? Christ when he went to the mountains knew what he was teaching us. On a mountain there is less gravity. We are farther from the Earth, and therefore we can more easily lift up our hearts. Now what actually happens in us?

In our psychology we also have a vertical element. We can go down to our subconscious and we can go up to the overconscious. Now I must be quite clear that the overconscious side of us implies the Kingdom of the Lord in us. The life of God in us. As Christ said again, "The Kingdom of God is in you. I and the Father will come down to you, and make a dwelling in you." So we have the Kingdom in us, but we are not conscious of it. We know that there is something very high in us—now I say *high* and you know why—but it is a sort of closed room. We only sometimes have glimpses into it through a small slit in the curtain that veils the overconscious side of our life.

We have also the subconscious side of our life and that means our vegetable life, animal life, emotional life—which is below the threshold of consciousness, and which contains tremendous richness. It can be compared to an iceberg in the sea; only one tenth is above water, nine tenths are below. You can see now that you have a subconscious, conscious and overconscious, three quasi-personalities I call them. Just as we have been created in the image of three persons, Father, Son and Holy Ghost.

Sometimes when you see a child playing about by himself, and talking to himself, you may say, "Well that's the first sign of insanity." It is not, ladies and gentlemen. One quasi-personality talks to another quasi-personality. Don't you find yourself sometimes talking to yourself? I talk quite often to myself and it helps me. Especially when I have a problem to think through. When I talk to myself, one personality talks to the other. It's an easy means of communication because our conscious side is not so much at home in the subconscious or overconscious.

Now the strange thing is that those three quasi-personalities, or three different sides to our life, were reflected in the Jewish Temple. Or the temple Moses built. You have the courtyard of the heathen, then the courtyard of the faithful, with men and women separated inside, and then you have the Holy of Holies, which is hidden by a curtain. Now what happened when Christ died? The curtain was shred into two. The Holy of Holies or the High Self, the life of God in us, was re-opened. You can enter again into the High Self. Now I can't talk here about the theological elements involved in this, because it's a tremendous subject. However you can see that the Jews, or Moses knew something about it. Consciously or subconsciously, I don't know. Or unconsciously because I would like to remind you that subconscious, conscious and overconscious can be divided into conscious and unconscious parts. Now the unconscious is above and below. For simplicity, following the kahuna psychological school I shall call the subconscious George and the overconscious Peter. Otherwise it's a mouthful to say. Now George and Peter are on both sides of our conscious life. The thing is, the kahunas knew all about our psychological structure for well over six thousand years. And about the overconscious, or High Self. You may have come across the books of Max Freedom Long about the kahunas. *The Secret Science behind Miracles* is the first book. The second book is rather foolish. The third book is very good again. They call the overconscious Aumakua, which means the good and benevolent father in us. Now that's exactly what we mean by the Father that dwells in us. It's a tremendous power, power quite uncomprehended by our mind, that makes us the adopted Son of God, of Himself. And the whole power of this position we owe to our contact with the High Self.

Now sacrifice has been a great problem for centuries. When I studied theology, and I went to different universities throughout the continent, speaking here and there, but nobody gave me an answer to why sacrifice is essential in our religion. All the books written about sacrifice don't give the answer – why?

The answer came when I encountered the explanation of Jacob's ladder. You might think, what's that dream to do with anything? Why Jacob's ladder? It's a very nice picture, but maybe he went round the bend. Look at it. Jacob is sleeping, dreaming. And because he is dreaming, the subconscious side of his life is involved. In sleep, the conscious side is not interfering. Now what happened? He is at the bottom of the ladder. On the top of the ladder is the Good Lord with His foot on the ladder. And there are angels going down and going up. Now what does this mean? It's a powerful metaphor for the subconscious contacting the overconscious through the conscious. There are angels coming down and going up. It means that our energy is circulating throughout mankind as such, through the three quasi personalities. Now what we call Original Sin is a twist in the ladder that prevents us from perfect contact between the subconscious and overconscious. Between George and Peter. A sacrifice was not required in Paradise. There was no sacrifice in Paradise. Why? Because the ladder was absolutely perfect. When energy was circulating, there was perfect resonance, as we call it in Physics. Perfect knowledge. And because of the perfect resonance, there is no loss of energy, and therefore we shouldn't die, we wouldn't be ill, we wouldn't suffer. We really could be king of nature. Commanding everything. We'll see why in a moment.

As a result of the twist, this power is blocked. The resonance is unbalanced. To use technical language, in an unbalanced electrical circuit, part of the energy must go back to the generator. In our case, Generator with a capital "G". And therefore, whenever we introduce a lack of balance into our psyche, we must lose energy, and for that, we must suffer and die. But the very moment that we are able to repair and restore the whole power in ourselves, we shall not suffer, we shall not die and we shall be completely free from gravity.

Another element which is very important is that Jacob's ladder was given to us in a pictorial way. How we ourselves can return to perfect harmony. Here we will come to prayer. If we look at the great teachers throughout human history, we find that they always teach in pictures. Our Lord in parables, and the others always refer to different kinds of pictures in order to impress us. Why pictures? Why are pictures important? Because they appeal to our imagination. What's all this imagination? After all we have will and reason. You may recall the words in St John's Gospel where he says that everything that has been created was created by the Word. Now what does that mean? The Good Lord had to have a picture of how his Word should appear and this picture was the element through which Creation came forth into being. So you can see that the imagination was a powerful creative force in the Lord's life, and the same thing happens in us. We should not refer to will power or brain power as the primary creative force, but refer to the power of the imagination, when it is perfectly obedient to the will and reason. If we can focus our imagination the right way, then the thing comes forth.

Perhaps you came across the books of Vincent Peale, *The Power of Positive Thinking*, or a book called *TNT - How to believe*. If you came across these books you will see from them how, when somebody wants to produce something he must concentrate on a picture and be absolutely firm in this picture, and then the thing happens. Shall I give you an example? Ten days ago I had someone suddenly call me, who first came to see me a year ago. He was a salesman. And we talked about different things. I spoke to him about *The Power of Positive Thinking*, the Vincent Peale book. When he returned later, ten days ago, shining, absolutely bright-faced, and with his wife—he introduced her to me—the first thing I noticed was his smooth walk. You could see the change in his manner, absolutely confident. He started talking, and said, "Well you know, yesterday I had six people from my firm, bothering me and asking me for six hours—What kind of formula do I use for selling?" He said, "I can't cope with all the orders. They are pouring into me. I just can't do it on my salary. It's too much work. The others are all selling very little." I said to him, "Did you give them the formula?" He said, "No. Vincent Peale pointed the way. I made the picture in my mind, that I sell. And I eliminated every negative thought from me. And the whole thing opened up for me. Like a stream of water."

Now if you get the books of Vincent Peale, you will see that on each page there's an example of that kind. In the United States when a big firm's sales fall, they call the board of directors and ask, "Who has a negative thought?" "Well I." "Go to church, start to pray and stop your negative thinking." In two weeks time business is booming again.

Perhaps you came across the Human Engineering Group, which discusses faith, and how faith can go on and produce things for you. It's more or less the same as Vincent Peale but they have made a psychological study of why faith works.

All this will give you a pictorial explanation of the power of our own self, so long as you stick to one picture, and you eliminate other, negative ones. If you want to achieve something and you still have something in yourself that says, "I may not achieve it," then you are done. And the best thing is to stick to one picture and not to bother any more about it. Let George and Peter work it out. They'll work it out beautifully. If you're worrying about it, then that means that you are not sure of achieving the aim and therefore you are putting up inhibitions. If you have inhibitions in your psychology, the whole thing doesn't crop up. In other words, if you say or if you pray for something through your conscious side and your subconscious side is just doing the opposite, it's exactly the same as two people dragging a rope, one in this direction and one in the opposite direction. And the result is a big zero.

We can now go into the problem of obedience of facts to our beliefs, or to our tension, or tendency. What does obedience mean? We usually understand obedience as, "Well I have to obey you, and you, or whatever you say. Yes mum, I'll do it." And I go on doing it till I get to God or someone at the top of the chain. But that's not obedience. Obedience means listening and looking to the laws of nature. An engineer who is building or drafting a new engine must very carefully obey the laws of nature; look for them, know them perfectly, and then he assembles the engine piece by piece, knowing the laws, making mathematically the whole structure of the engine. And when he obeys perfectly the laws of nature, then the laws of nature obey him. But if I want to start a car and someone tells me, "Well you have to start the starter." You say, "Don't tell me what I have to do. I want to push this button—the one for the lights." Nothing happens. Because I have to know the laws of nature, and when I obey them, or listen and look at them, and understand them, then nature will obey me.

Now you may understand the words in the Bible, "I shall not obey." Whatever the new perception is, it was this being who said, "I don't want to obey nature. I want nature to obey me. And they have to pull and push according to my will." But that's no good because you will not get any result out of it. Nature has its own framework of laws and you have to obey them. Now that means obedience. But this obedience has been twisted in our psychology by what we call Original Sin, when Eve took the fruit—I don't know who invented the apple—took the fruit and ate it. A very peculiar eating. Very important.

You can see now that by using your imagination you first have to obey; create a picture that will be in accordance with the laws of nature, outside yourself and inside yourself, and then you'll achieve something. In other words the insufficiency of knowledge is the first root of our prayer. Insufficiency of obedience. Once you have perfect knowledge, or perfect understanding, perfect obedience, then you can rule the world. But only then.

Now in order for us to get this perfect knowledge, obedience, understanding, we have to go back to this picture of the Low Self, Self and High Self. Or George, consciousness and Peter (subconscious, conscious and overconscious), and to the idea of sacrifice. In Paradise there was no sacrifice, because there was perfect knowledge. For instance, the Lord said, "You have to call the animals." Now imagine calling animals by name. You might say – you'll be the lion and you'll be the hare. *Onoma* in Greek, "name" in its ancient meaning means listening to the actual proportions of sound, or vibration in this person, in that person, in the lion, in the cat or in the hare. And when you listen to that name, you produce the sound with your mouth. You call the name of this person or tree or whatever it is. In your mind and with your mouth you reproduce the essential sounds. What will happen then? May I recall to you the story of Caruso. He got a little glass in his hand, and made it ring. He sang one octave higher than the sound, like a woman who sings one octave higher than a man, and the glass was shattered into pieces. Not into big pieces but into powder dust. He "called" the name of the glass. Now you can see that to call the name of somebody means listening, obeying, understanding the law of this particular nature, and then reproducing it by the power of your mind and body. That means to call the name. And when you call the name, you can move the object. The object will obey you. That is the basis for the legend of Orpheus. He could move trees. Mountains.

Back in the seventeenth century a man travelled throughout Poland, playing a flute. And whenever he entered any wood and started to play, all the animals would gather around, the hare, the fox, all sat listening attentively to his music. When he stopped, the animals went into the woods, without harming one another. And then the battle started again. When he came to the village, nobody could resist his music. Everybody came out, sitting and listening. He could call names, of people, animals. We have lost this power through the twist in our psychology. Therefore the sacrifice is essential.

What does it mean? The kahunas expressed it very well, that there must be a link between Peter and George. That we must take something from Peter, offer it to George, then George will transmute it and offer it to consciousness, and then it works. That's exactly what happens in any sacrifice. In my sacrifice, the sacrifice of the Mass, what I do is to take the bread, which symbolizes the offerings of people, like little grains of wheat, all collected into one bread; all the offerings, small or big, of the people. I take that; it doesn't need modification. You can offer anything, whatever you are joyful for, or thankful for, whatever you are changing in yourself. Everything is a matter for offering. Now I take this bread offer it to God, transmute it into blood and the flesh of Christ, and it comes back to me in Holy Communion. God doesn't need it for Himself. He wants only for us to do the right thing according to psychological law. That means to open the treasures from below, or open the treasures of Peter, extract from Peter whatever I want to produce, and offer that to the good Aumakua or the Lord above us. It is modulated by his tremendous light, and then it descends to us, and its radiance is consumed by our conscious self. As Christ said, the Kingdom of God is in us, is a treasure that you open and take new and old things out of. And remember that you must get through the big circle of High Self or Peter and then go down to your self. Because then you call upon two persons who have perfect knowledge.

Our George, the subconscious side, has a sort of radar arrangement with ourselves. Eastern teachings tell us that we are radiating something and this radiation encounters an object, is partly reflected, partly refracted, and partly absorbed. Now the part that is reflected comes to us and brings us the picture of the thing which we are trying to find out. Exactly like radar. The snag is that the picture coming to us is so weak that we need an amplifier in order to bring the whole picture into our consciousness. Clairvoyants have some sort of automatic amplification, and they can understand this information coming from outside. And mind you, there is no limitation to our imagination. I can go just now to my own home or my old home in Poland. Where I imagine I am, there I am. And I pick up radiation from there. But what happens? The input is too small. Why? I am accustomed to, and have been told and taught all my life that I can only see through my eyes and not through my brain. Then how do I see in my dreams? When you dream do you see with your eyes? There is a power in you to see, and not where the eyes are, but you don't use it. And if you don't practice, you don't get the power. The power is there. Wherever I go with my imagination, there I am. Though I can see the objects, normally they don't impinge on me. Why? Because my threshold of consciousness is too high and the input is too small. When I'm dreaming or sleeping, I'm not interfering and so the threshold of consciousness shifts down, and therefore the input can pierce through. But as it comes through the subconscious mind, it appears in different kinds of pictures which we have to interpret, as in psychoanalysis. However, can we lower our threshold of consciousness? And here I'll come in a moment to the supernatural side of prayer.

What is the threshold of consciousness? There are two things that raise the threshold of consciousness: selfishness and pride. When I love, what am I doing? In love I am going out from me to you. I'm trying to sense your desire. Feel what you want. I'm losing myself. I'm just not interested in me. I'm bored with myself. I'm interested in everybody around. And the more I'm interested in you, the more I feel what you want. I'm sensitive to you. But if I'm selfish, I build around myself a big wall and by Jove, you have to use some input to get through to me. Because I'm selfish. You see, love lowers the threshold of consciousness.

The other factor is humility. We have a very wrong idea about humility. It's like you say, "Well I don't know anything. I'm not good", and so on. It's sick pride. Humility is truth. Whatever I am, I am. Neither less nor more. A few days ago I gave an example about my father, because he exactly illustrates the point. My father was a very wealthy man, and once he went to a railway station. He wanted to travel to his home. He met a friend there. And the friend said, "Where are you going?" "I'm going home." "All right, we'll go together." My father said, "I don't know about that. Because you will go by first class and I will go by third." Well the friend looked at my father in confusion and said, "I didn't know you were such a snob."

Now you see, snobbery can be up and snobbery can be down. Pride can go up and pride can go down. But it's the same pride. Humility is truth. Whatever I am I am. Neither less nor more. Now if you have this kind of humility, a lack of pride, then you can completely dispense with yourself. By loving, you go out. And by annihilating yourself, you're prone to perceive every influence from outside. And that is the secret of clairvoyance. It's the understanding of people.

I've given you a few elements only, showing you the mechanical side as I call it, "mechanical" in quotes, of what happens in us and in surrounding nature when you start to pray. To "lift up your hearts". Now I've told you that the need for prayer comes from our consciousness of the insufficiency of our knowledge, our understanding. But there is still an insufficiency of our love. We have a tremendous pressure in our love, pressure which we cannot understand until we get a better light with which to see things. And in a moment I will return to this subject. First I have to tell you how to pray in order to understand.

If you look upon your own life, we are such as we imagine ourselves. The pattern of our imagination produces our character. Not only in individuals but in families, in nations. Now you have seen the power of imagination. What happens when you stick to one picture? It all depends what kind of picture you stick to. And this picture will influence your whole personality. You have to reach for the highest possible level in your imagination, in the pattern of your imagination, in order to understand and to obey in the sense of listening and looking. For that, you have to have light. So you have to use your imagination somehow so that you understand and you see, and that will give you the power, the possibility of loving; of relieving the tremendous pressure of inhibited love. Just now, you can't do it. You are shattered to pieces and you don't know how to love. You want to. Like modern rock and roll singers, they have all those uncontrolled emotions, because the pressure of love is so strong, but they don't know where to look for its release.

Now the answer to that is proper prayer. That means lifting up your hearts, or lifting your mind, towards light. You have to get to light. Now if your imagination is gloomy, then your self will be gloomy, negative, criticizing. Everything is wrong in life; everything is in the wrong position. You are on the wrong side of the stick and so on. But if your imagination is lit with light, you are cheerful, pleasant. You just see things.

A student of engineering once told me, "I remember when I was a small child, I could see in the darkness. Then people told me, and taught me throughout my school that I can't see in darkness. So I believed them, and then I couldn't see in darkness. But when I recalled this subject and I started to study the psychology of faith, then I brought back my faculty of seeing in darkness, so much so, that I could see in darkness as much as I can see in daylight." It happened because he brought light into being, into his visual power. And he said, "Also, after a while I could see through objects, and see inside them." Now that shows you what power you have if you bring light into yourself.

How is it done? When I start to pray, I first relax myself. Kneeling or not, it doesn't matter. Relaxed I imagine myself flooded with light. Not with natural light because it's a different kind of light. I mean Lucifer brings light but it's not the light of the supernatural being of Aumakua—the light which is in Peter. I don't want only the light of my subconscious self, the lower side of me. I want the whole light. So I reach immediately to my High Self, to Peter, and flood myself with the dazzling light of God. Shekinah, it's called in Hebrew. Now once you are familiar with that kind of prayer, and it will take you a few days or a few weeks, then you'll start to see things you never saw before. Because your imagination will form according to this light. It will change from darkness to light. From lack of knowledge to knowledge, because you will see. That is the law of nature. You have to go to the top of the ladder and there illuminate yourself. And that will work. It does work. Everybody whom I taught and who became a student of it found that it works unmistakably.

Once you are full of this light, you are obedient, which means you are receiving knowledge. And if you are obedient, not only to so-called dead objects—of course they are not dead, they're all alive, but never mind; if you're obedient not only to so-called dead objects, but to people, you start to understand them. And to understand people means to love. Now may I remind you, that in understanding or knowledge, its direction is from the object to me. Mathematically they call it a vector, a force with direction. Now if I absorb knowledge, I must be sensitive to what you have to tell me. Direction of information comes from you to my centre of information. But in love you have the opposite. I produce something which goes towards you. Now if I love somebody I start to identify with somebody. And the better I can identify with the object, the better I can understand it. And I can see through not only the surface. I can see what Plato called Ideas, the ultimate reality of the thing. But you must identify with it and for that you must love. If you absorb this fire, or light, you produce a sort of lens in yourself, and light the fire. I came to this world and want nothing else, only to light the fire. But the fire should be a blazing flame throughout the world, of love.

Now, if you produce that kind of prayer, then you not only understand people, but you can't help loving them. Whatever they are. Your enemies, your friends. But it's a different kind of love, something which embraces everything. Then you understand that to be absorbed in yourself is the most boring thing in life. It's hopeless to be busy with yourself. Because there are so many interesting things around.

Every one of us is a whole universe of boundless space. Taking only the physical side of it, you have atoms, so many, about ten followed by twenty seven zeros. Now every atom in itself is a planetary system. You can see that when you move in this universe of any of your quasi personalities you are in a vast, tremendous sort of temple where you can see the most beautiful things. All these atoms are interfering with their own radiation and your thought is modulated accordingly to your love or hatred. Sometimes I see people surrounded by not only radiation but beautiful patterns and different colours. You are surrounded by a tremendous sort of clothing, a garment of incredible light. And wherever there are crossings of radiation, there is a star, glowing and talking with different colours. And they are always harmoniously related to one another, if you are really loving. And that's beauty in itself. You can contemplate the whole thing and you will never be satisfied— if only *one* of you has seen it. The harmony of the universe is for ever around us but we have eyes and we don't see. We have ears and we don't hear because our hearts are hard, because we didn't step down in perfect obedience, and we didn't go up in perfect light. At the very moment that we combine the two together, the two extremes, Peter and George, obedience to the laws of nature, and the light which makes the power of the supreme being, then the fire is lit in you, and you begin to become a Man.

4

TOUCHING
THE DIVINE[1]

MacManaway: Andrew, I would like you to expand on what you describe as LLT.

AG: LLT stands for Love-Light Technique. It is a form of prayer, also an expansion of consciousness.

To understand it, first take a look at this representation of the Jewish Temple, built and given this shape by Moses, according to instructions given to him by God (Figure 2). Compare it to the structure of the human psyche (Figure 3-A). You have the courtyard of the gentiles, who don't know much about God. It represents darkness, corresponds to the collective subconscious; collective because all the heathen are there and all of nature is there. Then you have the courtyard of the faithful who know a little about the faith but not much. And then the individual subconscious, which you sometimes go into in dreams. Then you have the courtyard of the priests with two altars, love and intellectuality. Consciousness lies between the subconscious and overconscious—the Holy of Holies—from which it is separated by a curtain, representing the ego—the blockage we don't want light to penetrate. We want our own way of experimenting. The Holy of Holies represents the overconscious, or the light of God in us. Aumakua, as the Huna would call it, or the High Self.

39

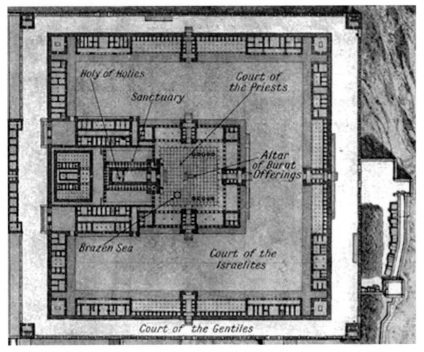

Figure 2: Detail of a Map of Solomon's Temple, circa 1000 BCE

Once you understand the parallel between the Temple and the two triangles, you know what to do. You have to part the curtain in two, in other words get rid of the ego and give way for the light of God to descend. When the light reaches the subconscious mind and the collective, you begin to be clairvoyant, able to see in one place or another place. But eventually more and more of this light comes through, and you are able to see and be aware of your field. The collective subconscious is your general field that penetrates the universe. So if you have no light there, that means no intellectual understanding, no awareness and no perception. Perception means light. Understanding.

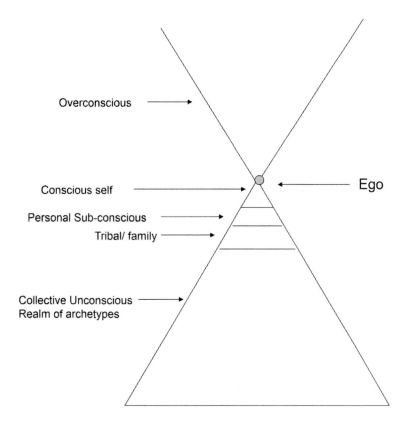

Figure 3–A: Diagrammatical view of the human psyche. Original State
The overconscious and conscious self are separated by the ego.

So what I call light, in my Light-Love Technique, means understanding—spiritual light, mental light which gives us the understanding of something. Now When you open up to it, the light will flood in, and instead of being like that (Figure 3-A), you will be like this (Figure 3-B). And once the light has totally penetrated, you are the perfect man. (Figure 3 – C), as you were in the primeval state of creation.

Figure 3–B: The human psyche—Intermediate State

By light I also mean intellectual light, or knowledge. Knowledge comes to us from outside our mind. Our mind accepts it; receives it. In love, it's your own self that goes toward the object you love. The two make a closed circuit. We start out, and we come back to the same point which everywhere in nature is the same; whether in electricity or magnetism, or any other sort of phenomena. We have a closed circuit. We have to expand both love and light; not only one.

The Love-Light Technique is a way by which I can expand my knowledge, and also expand and direct my love toward the object I understand. So that the more I identify myself with the object, the better I can comprehend it.

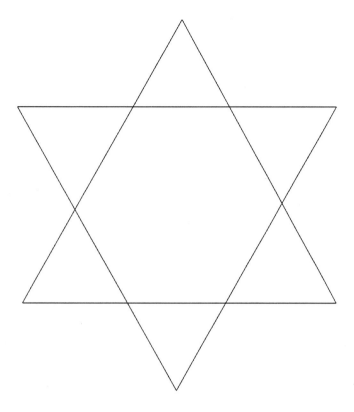

Figure 3–C: Representation of the perfect Man

If I would be the object itself, become the object, then I shall definitely understand the object properly, through and through.

Now once you grasp that, then consider the fact which is very commonly known, that repetition produces a perfect memory. If you want to remember poetry, instead of going around the room and trying to repeat the thing, sort of pounding it into your head, it's much easier if you read the poetry three times aloud to yourself. And then you put the book aside. After an hour or two—in between which you do something totally different—you read the poem three times aloud to yourself again. When you do it a third time after another hour, you'll find that you have nearly memorized the poetry. And the fourth or fifth time you really know it by heart so well that you'll know it for life. If you try to memorize the poetry, by repeating it, going around the room, you'll be able to recite the poem the way you might have done at school, but it's a sort of monotonous method of memorizing something.

The same sort of technique might be applied in the Love-Light Technique. What are you actually doing? You are opening yourself completely to light and love. You have to understand that, however you see yourself thus you become. If a youngster sees himself as a famous engineer, makes the effort to see what he is able to become, he will open a channel and he will actually achieve his goal. Because he sees a picture and the picture will eventually become his reality. So, in the Love-Light Technique you have to visualize yourself as full of light, a longing light. That also means love. The fire of love. I have in mind of course not ordinary light but the light that comes from the supernatural being of God and His light. Now if you repeat that constantly, then eventually the penny drops and extraordinary things start to work in you.

Sit in a chair, and see yourself flooded with light. If you can do it, imagine yourself sunbathing on the beach of God where the light of God reaches you and penetrates you through and through, and lights the fire inside you, so that it starts to burn. Make this picture in yourself, so that you can see it properly. It may take you some time to begin with. The first day you sit in your chair relaxed, start to believe in it, and then you'll see yourself as I said, sunbathing in the light of God and then this light will start to burn in you like a fire. Eventually, the second time you do this, the third or after a week, the picture will be familiar to you and you won't need to spend much time re-opening the picture. You'll sit down and immediately the picture will be there, present in yourself.

Once you grasp that, you can repeat the picture hundreds of times in a day. You walk, you talk, you go to the pictures, you dance, you sit or you go to sleep, you can recreate this picture, and by virtue of the creation of this picture, the penny drops. Eventually the light comes in and starts to illuminate different compartments of your self, the collective subconscious. The light from the top triangle penetrates into the bottom diagram. Both triangles are collective. The top one is the collective overconscious, the community of awareness in the field of God, of all Creation, and the bottom one is the awareness of all Creation that you have within yourself. Now by repeating the Light-Love Technique, you open a respective channel in the collective unconscious and in your individual subconscious, so that light can penetrate there. The threshold of consciousness starts to lower, and permits your consciousness to see in that light, and gradually you start to enlarge your awareness of the vast possibilities you have within yourself.

The Greeks said, man, know thyself and thou shall know the universe. Because actually the collective unconscious is the whole universe; being a collective, it belongs to all of us. But because there's darkness, because there is no conscious light there, we don't see anything. The practice of LLT introduces light into the triangle of your subconscious. That is what I call the development of Field Awareness by introducing the light of God.

You can do it without the light of God. Like a diver going below the surface, you will see fish or plants, the life of the underwater, but the very moment you put a searchlight there, the same light which is green and brown, shines with a tremendous array of colours. Now the same thing happens when you dip your consciousness into the collective unconscious by introducing the light of God and the love of God. The point is that when you introduce the light, you can see in it, and admire what you see. But when you introduce love you start to identify yourself with the object, in the sense that your attention is identified, with a particular star, or an insect or whatever it may be.

Temporarily you can focus two thousand years in the past, on a certain person, and through love, identify yourself with that person. You can actually live the life of that particular person. I think that is absolutely in line with Christian doctrine. There's nothing against it. But it doesn't mean that the whole of your personality is identified with that object. It means only that for the time being, on that day you are focused on it. Because the collective unconscious is outside space and time, as a result of your field you can partially identify with that object. But you can also withdraw your focus and go somewhere else. By doing so, you can develop your consciousness; which means going from one level to another. Regarding reincarnation, I think the concept will eventually be shown to be correct, but much deeper than the commonly held view that I have been this or that person. That view limits you to a little being instead of "a being without limit", the whole universe at once.

You limit your field with ordinary conceptions as with information. People do so now. They limit themselves to the body, which is nonsense. You have to be unlimited. Practically unlimited as concerns space and time. But you can focus yourself in a certain part of space. Now if you repeat LLT, Love-Light Technique for a certain time, perhaps you will not notice any change. But others will notice one when they see you from time to time. That your sensitivity has increased, that you are much more cheerful, much freer, that you are much quicker in your perceptions. You become witty, a very good mixer. Simply because when you introduce light into the deep strata of the unconscious mind, you start to see and you rid yourself of fear of the unknown. The more you know, the less you are afraid of what you don't know. The knowledge might be sometimes blurred, sometimes it might be only partial. But as your knowledge increases, so your freedom also increases, and your lack of fear. And when you rid yourself of fear, you find absolute, perfect joy. And that I think is heaven. And if you can achieve that through LLT, in this lifetime without dying, then you will not die. You'll just pass to another level.

MacManaway: You slide between levels?

AG: Yes. Obviously by LLT you expand yourself. You are incapable of selfishness. You also are so taken with the world outside yourself that you have no time for it. It's boring to be concerned with yourself because you are so busy with other things outside yourself. And that is the technique. I call it a technique in order to fit with modern conceptions, especially of young people. They love all sorts of technical things. But that's what I call prayer. The essence of prayer is not only talking. That's not its meaning. But it's touching; actually experiencing the immense presence of the infinite. And I call it Divine Sex, because it's the act of touch. There's a spiritual sense of touching. But you have to be Field Aware. I consider Field Awareness as a very thin radiation going throughout my universe: my particular pattern, my personality, my basic tone. And through this radiation I am in touch with the tremendous radiation of the universe. And that is a tremendous thrill. That sort of in-touchment with the Supreme is the essence of prayer. Prayer means being in contact with your field. It's not connected with talking. As in meditation, the less you talk the better you meditate. The better you are in touch with him. Because it's a trust. A joy. Submission to the Supreme. You cease to exist and He exists. As St John the Baptist said, "I have to go and He has to stay". You diminish to nothing and He increases to infinity in you. Now that is part of an act of prayer that can be achieved, in a comparatively short period of time by LLT. The more often you repeat Love-Light Technique the faster you progress in spiritual growth, awareness of your field.

When you combine LLT, the awareness of your field and meditation, progress is very rapid, in comparison with the sort of progress that St Teresa describes in her work on meditation or John of the Cross who mainly talks about darkness. There you plod along.

Light is so invigorating that in it you start to see a totally different world. A world that is outside of the shapes of things we normally see. Actually, to begin with, you see the etheric world, that is, the Ideas of

Plato. You see the interlacing connections of the field, of the atoms and molecules, all shining with light. Glittering with stars. It's a fairy world. No words can describe what you see when you go into the Ideas. But these Ideas are only the first step. Then you go into the Ideas of the Ideas. That is the after world. And you go further up. Eventually you land in a world of indescribable beauty, and indescribable joy which any words fail to describe. And that is the prayer, which through LLT you can reach comparatively quickly.

Divine in-touchness may throw some light on the problem of sex that we are so much involved in, in this so-called permissive society. Recall the two triangles I drew, the upper and the lower (Figure 3-A). In Jung's conception, which you may want to study further in his books, consciousness is always the opposite sex to the subconscious. That means, that if your conscious is male your subconscious is female. And as the Huna school calls the subconscious life George, that means that I have Georgina not George. Now we have some sort of intuition, that in our collective subconscious the whole knowledge of the universe is contained. Therefore instinctively we have a drive toward the collective subconscious, to grasp all knowledge that is there at our disposal. But the threshold of our consciousness is so high that we can't get to that knowledge. Yet we have a drive towards it. Because our subconscious is of the opposite sex, intuitively we suppose that the opposite sex will give us the knowledge we seek.

In Paradise, after the Fall, the first parents went to the bushes and covered their loins because they felt a drive. The drive was sex. Now it could be interpreted that they were feeling a drive toward their own subconscious, so they might understand what had happened there. But because the light was withdrawn, the top triangle had withdrawn, and they'd lost access to that knowledge. Everything was dark. Therefore the drive that Adam felt, instead of being directed towards the subconscious, was directed at the conscious side of the woman, because the woman was of the opposite sex to his consciousness. Previously they didn't feel that drive because they had full knowledge, a union with the subconscious mind, whereas after the Fall when the light had gone out and the threshold of consciousness was raised, they wanted badly to unite with each other, to marry their own subconscious minds. In psychology it's known as the phenomenon of transference. You transfer the drive, the nostalgia for perfect knowledge, perfect love and perfect peace, to the woman, expecting that she, being the image of the subconscious mind will supply that knowledge.

From that it would appear that the sex drive of a man toward a woman results from nostalgia for Paradise lost, expressed in the lateral instead of the vertical. In the state of perfect knowledge a man will still have a drive towards a woman because she is, in her structure opposite to his structure. We shall have the desire for union, but it won't be so strong and it won't be in both directions.

Now we have to realize from the Old Testament where God speaks to the Jews that "I'm your husband and you are my wife", and in the same context St Paul says it of Church and Christ, it means that the top triangle is male compared to the bottom triangle. Which is also expressed in the Bible where it says that the Earth will open up and the rain will come and the Earth will produce cereal. The top triangle pushes into the lower triangle and brings light. The Earth of the lower triangle, the wife of God opens herself up to receive the seed from above and produce a new child, a child of God; as in Baptism. It doesn't mean that a new physical child is born. It means that the same child which has been born human becomes deified through Grace, through union with God. Through a perfect marriage with God.

In that respect, we have to understand all the sayings of the Bible about Redemption as being a marriage. The supreme marriage is accomplished in the relationship of God and humanity, and through humanity all of Creation. And that is what St. Paul says in the Letter of the Ephesians Chapter 5, that Christ and the Church constitute a marriage union. When God speaks of Israel, Israel represents humanity. We are in union with God and through that union we acquire Redemption. That is, we are lifted up to the participation of divine nature, of divine Grace. And here you also have a parallel to sex, the drive for sex and desire, but it is sublimated. It is what I call Divine Sex, when through prayer you are in touch with God. Now, from that it is clear how sex is very sacred. And I think, due to certain influences of the Manichean heresy, also influences in the Jewish tradition, sex was always seen as dirt, which is totally wrong. It is as sacred as God. It is life-force, natural life-force. When that light force is mingled with the light of God, through Grace we are then able to produce children of God.

Christ being married to humankind radiates Grace throughout Creation, throughout humankind giving birth to new children, the children of God. He spoke about that in St John's Gospel, Chapter 3, to Nicodemus, when he said that unless a man has been reborn he cannot enter the Kingdom. Now strange enough divine Grace is like water, like divine raindrops, a divine dew. Grace is really water, and in this water and through divine Grace you have to be reborn in the Holy Spirit, which means in perfect love of Godhood. We not only accept the knowledge of this universe, but we also accept the love of God toward the universe. That love is the real love of the husband to the wife. So you see there are parallels to marriage in the Bible, parallels where the Redemption is seen as the marriage between God and humanity; a perfect union, a perfect penetration of divinity and humanity, and through that, of all Creation.

5

LOVE,

MARRIAGE AND SEX[1]

A G: We all know what love is. And if I ask you what it is, what
would you say?
(Inaudible response.)
AG: No. it is resonance. Being in resonance.

If I love somebody I am trying to be one with them. With him, with
her, with this or that, and the more I can unify myself with the object,
the better I comprehend the object. If I unify myself with this chair
down to the last atom, I shall have all knowledge of this chair, and I
will know exactly everything about this chair: where the wood comes
from, how it grew, who cut it down, who made it out of the timber, who
supplied it and so on. The whole knowledge of it will come to me. I will
fit into the field of the tree and therefore the whole history of the tree
will be perfectly understandable to me. Now that is what we have to be.
We have to draw light into the Earth. Therefore the whole technique
of prayer is not only to open oneself to the light but at the same time
as the light comes to me, to light the fire. That means to direct myself
towards the field, and the field not only of understanding but the field
of wisdom, that means loving. Being in resonance.

When I strike a tuning fork here, and an instrument with a string
stands over there, the string will respond. Now that is resonance between two patterns of life, that means between man and woman, between man and an object, man and a plant. And if I am in resonance,
then when I change as a result of any problem, the resonating field

will immediately advise me that there is something wrong with the resonance. That's how the plant will immediately know that I am not well, because in that case the plant cannot be in resonance with me, and won't be. You follow then, how the Field Theory explains quite a lot of things.

Now this resonance of the field brings not only understanding, that means a conception, but also resonating, meaning that my whole essence is one with the tune. It's a sort of treble and bass accompaniment in music. The right hand plays the tune and left hand plays the background. Strange enough here you have the sensation of man and woman, bass and treble. But they have to be in unison in the same key. In modern music it's different; you have several keys and therefore you can feel the dissonance. But here, you have to bring in light and love, that is understanding and resonating, and then you experience a perfect closed circuit. Your energy goes up, and comes back to you. There is a perfect feedback, and this feedback immediately reinforces your personal vibration. Therefore you can grow.

Therefore with any man who really loves a woman, or a woman who loves a man, they usually grow better and not worse. If they are in perfect resonance. If not, if the resonance is limited to the body and doesn't extend to the spirit, they may deteriorate because there is more and more distance between the two; in their tuning. If it is only spiritual and not a physical resonance, there may be also dissonance but we'll see shortly that it is not so. Because the love between man and woman is a most peculiar phenomenon, and it's this sacrament, that is much more important than the Eucharist. To begin with, this will come as a shock to the theologian, but eventually he will say, "You're quite right. Why didn't we see it?"

For fifteen hundred years marriage was seen as a necessary evil. Because they thought that sex was an evil force. That it's dirty. And then at the Grand Council of Trent, marriage was defined as a sacrament, that means, a means of sanctification. Reluctantly, but it was derived from the Bible. They accepted it but still persisted in their view that after all the perfect state is the virginal state. Eventually, they've come to the conclusion that sex is not necessary filth.

In any sort of relationship between man and woman, when they are attracted to one another, there is a certain radiation between the two, a certain excitement, mental, physical or spiritual. There is a certain excitement of the life force. No doubt about it. The in-touchness of two fields stimulates the life force to be active. Now this life force is usually radiated away. If you put a pendulum in front of a man who has drunk a lot, you will find that the pendulum makes all sorts of fantastic movements. He loses energy. Energy pours out of him, it doesn't come back and therefore next day he has a hangover. Because he has lost too much energy. In sex the life energy goes out but should come back from the other partner. And then it's a closed circuit, and there is no hangover, provided there is the right love. Now love—the life force, can be represented as a circle, going out and coming back. But in the course of a lifetime of growing consciousness, beliefs of different kinds constellate. There's the belief that I can't see in darkness and therefore I put up blockages against my sensitivity to infra-red. And then I don't see in darkness. Another blockage for example is that I can't stand this or that food. All those sets of beliefs grow within my circulation of energy. Eventually the life force has to force itself more and more through those blockages. As time goes by, the amount of my blockages increases and eventually the life force cannot pass through them. We become senile and we die. Because we don't get our energy back. The energy goes out to the Generator (with a capital "G").

You may have seen a program on TV called "The Human Jungle"[2], where Doctor Corder, a psychologist, solves the problems of different women. Invariably the woman falls in love with the psychologist because he releases one of her complexes. She is so relieved to be so free that she sees this man as her redeemer. He is the one who brought her salvation. Poor Doctor Corder is in a terrific dilemma because he hasn't got any romantic feeling toward this woman, but she has become crazy about him. And then comes the husband who starts to make scenes about it, and stops the woman from being cured. The woman goes back to the husband. The doctor somehow goes back to the man, the plot becomes complicated and eventually the woman is relieved of her complex. After a few months she is also relieved of her love for Doctor Corder. She goes back to her husband, but she is a totally different person. And Doctor Corder says, "Thank God I'm free."

Now something of this kind should go on in a marriage, because the man is not affected by the same association of the blockage that the woman has. They may have the same blockage but their mental associations are different. Therefore my radiation going out to my partner also contains my blockages, but the partner doesn't accept them and sees through them. Only the true radiation gets through; the rest is stopped and rejected. The true radiation from the partner comes back to me, uncontaminated by blockages. And because I have been relieved of my blockages, I fall in love with the partner. The secret of permanent love is that the partners have to solve each others' blockages, one after the other, through the flow of vital force from one to the other, where each partner sees the blockage of the other partner and rejects it.

Rudolf von Urban wrote the book *Sex Perfection*[3] which is mostly sex business and not very interesting, but there are two cases really of interest, one of an "electrical" girl and one of a neurotic girl.

A married couple are fantastically in love. After marriage, they are naked together, lying on a bed. There's no intercourse, but they are absolutely happy. But when they stand up, the man sees his wife in a halo of fiery light. He approaches her and sparks pass between them. He is terrified, because of the electric shock. So he goes to the doctor to ask his advice. The doctor is very interested, because he is a psychologist and a doctor and a physicist. He asks the man to repeat the experiment in different ways, to find out when the radiation stops, when it emerges and so on. This is one case.

The other case is of a neurotic girl. A beautiful blonde girl is terrified of men. If a man is in the same room with her she starts shaking. She can't stand the presence of men. None of the famous psychologists that she consulted can find the root of her problem. She'd tried analysis with various psychologists and eventually she ends up in the clinic of Doctor von Urban where the only personnel are women. There are no men except for him and a young doctor who is in charge of the clinic. She is sent there as a deputy secretary to do some typing. To begin with she is very uncomfortable with the presence of the younger doctor, but eventually she gets accustomed to him so that he doesn't affect her. They still can't find the root of her problem. The young doctor falls in love with the young girl, but cannot win her as she can't stand the presence of any men. But after two years she is not only accustomed to him, but she starts to sympathize with the young man. Eventually she agrees to marry him on condition that there won't be any intercourse between them. He agrees to that because he is terribly in love with this girl.

They marry, and after six weeks of marriage they finally go to bed together. He's had several affairs with different women and he knows all about love, physical love, but she doesn't know anything. He has to fight in order to keep his promise. They lie beside each other. After half an hour they realize that something terrific is happening between them. They don't know what it is but it grows and grows, and they sense a flow. They reach an ecstatic state and eventually, after several hours, they cannot stand it, so they have to get up, take a bath and rub themselves with some wet towels. Because the ecstasy is too great. Later on they described it as something out of this world. Time didn't exist. They were in a different world altogether. He said he'd never felt such happiness in his life. They go to Rudolf von Urban who does various experiments, and he comes to certain conclusions. The ecstatic state goes on for fifteen years. After fifteen years they have their first intercourse. This state disappears and never comes back. Rudolf von Urban concludes that the couple experienced Platonic Love that Greeks knew about, but about which all knowledge has since been lost. Probably other couples experience it too but they never talk about it. For couples this experience is repeatable. And that is real love.

In accordance with the field theory, I wrote a paper on the theology of marriage, around 1957 and sent it to Rome, but received no comments. I used a pseudonym because I didn't want to be pestered by being called to Rome to do further researches. That's not my job. So I wrote under the pseudonym, Paul Brother. I sent it to my bishop. My bishop knows who wrote it, but he cannot publically review it. So I am safe. Anyway, the story is this. I started by analyzing marriage from the point of view of the Bible. The teaching of the Church is that marriage is a sacred thing and that its purpose is the procreation of children. Now if the church taught that for hundreds of years here is the puzzle.

In Genesis, after the Fall God turns to Eve and tells her, "I will multiply your pains *and* your conceptions." Not "*in* your conceptions" as some of the translators wanted to put it. It's obviously a twisting of the Bible. The Hebrew text, the Greek text and the Latin text all have "and" and not "in". Theologians call it a sort of symbolic language but it is not. What does it mean? It's a curse, and not a blessing. It means that the woman cannot control her conceptions.

Further in the Bible we see that the relationship between God and Israel is a marriage relationship. So said the prophets, "I'm your husband, you are my wife. You're unfaithful to me because you go to other gods." Also God said to Hosea, "Go to this town. You'll find a married woman. Take her as a partner and you will produce living children. That is a living picture of the relationship between me and Israel." The betrothal is on Mount Sinai, and then the marriage. And it goes on and on. The same is repeated in the New Testament. Christ says, "The Kingdom of God is like a wedding party." St Paul picks up the same theme, especially in his letter to the Ephesians. In Chapter 5 he says that the relationship of Christ and the Church is a marriage. And other marriages have to conform to it. And it's not just words. He means what he says. And you have the second letter to Corinthians, Chapter 11, "I have married you as a pure virgin to Christ, as a new man. And I am the groom's best friend, the best man."

Now what follows from that? To begin with, what is the aim of the marriage between God and Israel? Is it the procreation of children? Obviously not. It's to multiply the children of God through the redemption of Israel and to bring them to God. Christ repeats that in his speech to Nicodemus when he says, "If somebody is not reborn of water and the Holy Spirit he will not enter the Kingdom." The greatest marriage that ever existed is the Incarnation. God nature takes human nature, two of them into one partnership, one person. They are two in one. And the purpose of this marriage, the supreme marriage is what? It's redemption. The radiating away of the love of these two, married into unity. And therefore every marriage should conform to this marriage, of the Incarnation. And it's obvious from what I said that in every marriage there is this natural phenomenon of ecstasy, of life-force, on which and only on which the life force of God can be superimposed and distributed. Because Grace never destroys nature but builds upon nature. Therefore whatever Grace has to do it does it through natural laws. So the Grace of the over-conscious must marry the unconscious, which is just the Incarnation as you see here, where the bonds of self have been broken. Christ as perfect Man is a perfect marriage where the radiation of the life-force of natural phenomena is the foundation upon which the supernatural marriage of God and humanity is accomplished.

Hence the first and primary aim of marriage is redemption. Like Christ's Incarnation was a redemption. As Christ took on the complexes of human beings on himself and gave his wife the resurrection, so also the partners both have to do the same, in circulating energy of one to the other. Therefore the prime aim of marriage is children—spiritual children. Not physical.

The second aim of marriage is the longevity of both parties, because senility comes from different blockages. If the partner can solve my block, then the partner brings me true revival, true freedom. I can breathe and energy starts to work in me again. The field starts to create, and therefore the life forces return to me and don't go out to the Generator. As in a wireless with a resonant circuit, if there isn't perfect resonance, part of the energy goes back into the power source. If there is perfect resonance there's no loss of energy. Actually such a thing doesn't exist as heat is emitted through the wires, and that is a loss of energy. But in perfect resonance, the energy lost from the mains is very small. There is no heat loss. I told you that heat is one of the primary things about us. You follow? It links all things together. And therefore in a perfect marriage where two people love one another in resonance, their union brings out their complexes, and they solve them and they never lose energy. Therefore they permanently reduce their senility, returning to normal activity, apparently twenty-five or thirty years old. And they never age beyond that. There is no death. They can go to the next level, and then they disappear lock stock and barrel from one level to appear on another level. We haven't reached that state yet. Except for Elijah and Enoch in Old Testament. Those are two cases. There are two cases in the Old and New Testament of physical trans-ference from one place to another: Daniel being fed by Habakkuk and Philip who was taken to the town of Azotus, in Acts. Those cases are of physical transference. But the only two cases that concern transfer-ence from one level to another are of Enoch and Elijah.

Now you can see that the relationship between man and woman must be primarily a field relationship, and not a physical relationship. The physi-cal may come in as the third possible connection, but it may ruin the first two completely, as in the case told by Rudolf Von Urban of the neurotic girl. And in that case it would be a sacrifice to have a physical relationship with one another. Because that means a danger of losing that fantastic, ec-static state that you had acquired. But we maintain a set of beliefs, habits inborn in us, that the only, primary purpose in marriage is sexual. Once we switch off that set of beliefs we see that the physical relationship is not the main purpose, and it may lead to calamity. You start then to think in terms of resonance, of spiritual communion, of spiritual orgasm, of spiri-tual communion of your field with God. I call it Divine Sex. When you start to touch the field of God, it's a question of in-touchness. And that's what they call prayer. Meaning resonance with Him.

You can be in such a perfect marriage with God, with plants, with women, with men, with anybody. Often there is no outer indication of it. Very often we don't even know that we have a relationship of such kind with this man or that woman. For goodness sake don't spoil it with any sort of physical tangent, because you will ruin the relation-ship. You will lose the thrill of tremendous love that comes from the heart, of being totally one with the whole environment.

Sometimes young girls fall in love with me, and just want to be con-stantly with me. I said to one, "My dear child, I love you tremendously. I love you so much, with infinite love. As God loves you so I love you too. She looked at me and said, "Oh no, how dare you!" I said, "That's my love, and the reason for life is His love; as much as He loves the little creatures. You want by your love to be possessive of me. I don't know how. It won't give you peace because you are afraid of losing me. You want me to love only you, and therefore you narrow yourself to a certain limit. I give you my love. In that love the ego is gone, your life is free because you are married to Creation." She got all upset. She wanted to marry me. I replied, "Dear child I am married already to Creation, so I cannot marry you. I'm sorry. Even so, I could not marry you. That's my life. And I would want to teach you the same love." After a certain time she started to understand, and she said, "Now I am free, and this love is so beautiful. It gives you a feeling of serenity, and I can go now and love another boy and still have the background of your love." I replied, "I would not want anything else." And now she understands and said to me, "You are a totally loving person, of freedom and peace."

Sometimes when I talk about such things, at meetings or church fellowship, somebody says to me, "What can you know about love? You are Roman Catholic and not married." And I say, "I beg your pardon, it's my profession. And you can't tell me that I'm not a professional lover." "What kind of love?" "Ah this is a thing to discuss. And this sort of love has nothing to do with the physical love that you have in mind, that involves jealousy." There is no jealousy in this love. There is no possession. Only giving. And if I in my profession fall in love in perfect resonance, and a girl tells me, "I want to go with another man as I will be happy with him," I will be overjoyed. I will say to her, "Go and have him. Because the only love I have is for you to be happy and not for me to protect you, using you as an instrument for my happiness."

So love as you can see now, and I just touch upon it, is a resonance of fields, and such love has to be your resonance to the great field of the universe, to mankind, that means your subconscious mind, and the great love of the overconscious which is collective too, and belongs to everybody around. Like Grace it goes from me to Anna and from me to Sylvia and to Bruce and to Bill and then to Ludi and Barbara and so on. It grows like the sap in a particular plant, from cell to cell. And if the cell closes itself, it dies and the plant is deprived of further food. So we must pass love on, and then go on in in-touchness with the whole of Creation, imagining your love as a tremendous field, of many tendrils, Aka Chords the Huna would say, touching the whole of Creation, millions of them, resonating, and bringing all that to the supreme field which is His, resonating with Him as an offering.

It's not a sacrifice in the sense that I suffer for this. He, Christ has taken all the pain of it. I once asked Christ to give me all the pains of everyone, provided that everyone would be happy. I'm offering myself to take everyone's pain provided everyone would be safe. But He said, "Oh no. I have done it. You can't do it a second time. Sorry, I reserve for you the joys, and not the pains." And if you find one place in the Bible where Christ asks you to multiply your crosses every day, then I shall give you twenty-five quid. It's not much, a little for me. He always says—meet the crosses of the day and when you meet them with love, the crosses vanish. There's no cross. If I love somebody there's no cross for me. And what a joy it is. Because I love. And when you love Creation, there is no pain. Because the very moment that you are in pain, it's gone. You are happy that you can do something for Creation. So you see, real love brings you to joy, peace and serenity. And you are in contact with Creation and in contact with God.

6

MEDITATION[1]

You ask if the essence of Meditation is the opening of oneself to God, and whether this can only be achieved in complete relaxation of one's whole being. Yes. Now only God can really open all your mind and heart to Him. *You* can't; but He gives you the impulse to try and when you obey it, in answer to your effort towards Him, God then does the opening for you, and goes on opening you to the point where He can take complete charge of you. This may take time, and be imperceptible to you. Spiritual growth is hidden from our seeing - just as you did not see yourself growing when young. God opens our shutters when we begin to try to open them ourselves. Then His love and Light can pour in for you to absorb, because this Grace pours out all the time on everything, everywhere, and is unlimited.

The human personality has a central point of its being. The art of going to this central point is to relax yourself completely and to plunge deep down into yourself. Some call it the "ground of the soul", others the "high point of the soul", but it is the central point of the personality as such. When you reach this point next you have to pass to the overconscious, through which the Grace of God pours down, and you relax in Light and Love. When you reach this point, you go one step further, into the chamber of God, where God dwells in you. He is the Supreme Being, and you are only a created being. When you get there you expand yourself, open yourself completely in total communion, without any pictures. You are like a bar of iron in the fire. It becomes

61

incandescent and disappears wholly from sight, but remains iron. You make contact. You rest in God. There is complete silence. You understand why they call God, Nirvana. It is not "nothing". It is complete silence, where you are absolutely nothing in comparison with Him.

Now, in this you have to find your own way of meditation. As a child you start with pictures, but as you grow up you introduce Him into your consciousness as such. Light, fire, or love it may be, but never any anthropomorphic representation. Once that is achieved you have dismissed the pictures of your childhood, and you want to let God take over and deal with you, to concentrate on nothing in complete relaxation. It is a good thing to repeat a single word - an opening word that has meaning and sound, such as "Thou", and which is an outgoing affirmation of a presence, of contact. Whatever energy you receive from God in your Meditation you must never, never keep for yourself, but immediately must distribute to your whole environment.

Our repeated mistake is visualising ourselves as being inside the body, and thinking inside the brain. We have to learn to visualise ourselves as a field covering tremendous spaces, where there is perfect knowledge in communion and union with God. We must visualise ourselves at the perimeter of our field, which is large beyond all conception, whose lines converge on our body-mind. All our thinking and feeling takes place in our field, and not in the brain, which is simply our wireless set, our transformer.

How we see ourselves, that we tend to become; not what we see in the mirror but what we habitually imagine ourselves to be. So you must imagine yourself out in space, your field spread over the universe. Here you are in contact with the Supreme, and you will experience a feeling of immense freedom for you are not tied to your body, and in this freedom you can relax a million times better than in any other way.

Your personality is simply a set of proportions forming a unique pattern. There are consequently millions of different patterns of personalities, of fields throughout the universe like thousands of radio waves mingling together, from which you can select what you want if you have an instrument with which to tune in. You can tune into one or other of the millions of personalities, of fields.

It is essential to visualise your body as a physical set of proportions, a pattern of proportions which obviously you can see. The centre of your personality is a set of spiritual proportions, governed by the virtue of prudence (or wisdom) that balances all spiritual proportions. Learn to visualise yourself as this field which covers immense spaces. Your spiritual nature is beyond space and time, and therefore it may be in one place, or anywhere in the universe; it matters not.

In planetary systems the astronomical bodies are located relative to one another in a set of proportions that arises from the tension in space, gravitation. This tension regulates their motions. Exactly the same thing occurs in the atomic world. So it is not a question of size but of proportions. In fact they are known to be always musical proportions. The moment in meditation that you concentrate on a set of proportions you are in a different dimension. We are given our basic set of proportions—our basic musical theme, and the problem of our life is how to develop that theme, how to combine and compose our life; because it is a whole composition. We can either compose it as pop music or a symphony. We are placed in the world which we conceive through our senses, but being outside time and space, we are one step nearer the Kingdom; but one step only—in the antechamber of the antechamber of the antechamber of the Kingdom. Then gradually you approach the antechamber, and eventually you are in the Kingdom. And then you are somewhere that is quite beyond description. You fit into the whole universe, and the whole universe is in tune with you, and therefore your slightest movement affects the motions of the surrounding environment, which is not of size but of proportions. (e.g. Blake's "thou can'st not pick a daisy without troubling a star"). There is an indescribable harmony in which your whole personality is emotionally in tune. It's inexpressible: a fragrance, a light, a display of fruits, of colour, of water-music. It feeds you, fills you and is beyond this world's conception. No words can express what you will start to feel when through the central core of your personality you are able to enter into meditation, through which you eventually achieve the goal and enter the Kingdom.

Is the way there by desire? No. By love, and not that which arises from yourself, but through Grace which is given to you freely. Sanctifying Grace is just like the rays of the sun. It falls upon all, everywhere, and is plentiful, but we are closed. We close our shutters for we are afraid of this light. As I said, open yourself completely, for that is our work, by God's help to open ourselves wholly to light and love. Then light and love will pour in, and start to take charge of you. Gradually God takes you into His hands and completes the work of sanctification in you.

This meditation is first by relaxation, which is the opening of the shutters; then by visualising yourself as an open bowl filled completely from every side, so that light and love penetrate you completely, absolutely, utterly. Thus freed from all other considerations you give God the possibility to take complete charge of you, and direct you. That is the goal of meditation—the whole goal. Do not return to visualising the concerns of your daily life, and making earnest resolutions as is so often urged in spiritual books. Yes, at first thoughts will wander back to these anxieties, but gradually they will cease. Often a brief prayer or the Divine Name will be enough to bring you back to undisturbed concentration. Yes, I think the Orthodox Church's "Prayer of Jesus" is lovely for this if used as an invocation. Whatever you use must be short, for the heart of meditation is silence. This is essential to meditation, for only in the heart of silence will you find God.

Meditation is communion with the Supreme, and that only.

7

THE HOLY TRINITY[1]

We've talked about the one nature of God, conscious of himself. I am who I am. He[2] is His existence whereas the created has His existence. Which means it is not in the nature of the created being to exist. The nature of God is that He is the existence of Himself. I am who I am. Now that is his nature as one, a complete unity.

Now there are two active processions[3] in God. What does procession mean? Christ spoke of a Father and a Son. Now, we're back again to a sort of analogy of fatherhood and filiation. Because when he was talking to people he had to use some sort of representation of what was going on with the actual nature of God. God didn't actually marry. The person we are talking about has an awareness of himself, and of his love. In order for him to be aware of that he has to conceive the picture of himself. He has to be aware of himself as such. For example if I want to conceive and understand a car I have to produce a picture of the car in my mind. Now the picture of the car in my mind is absolutely united with my mind. But it is not my mind. It is something produced by my mind. It is conceived by it, a procession, a picture from my mind. Now if I conceive myself, if I am able to conceive myself, then I shall have a picture of myself, that gives me a procession, gives me a sort of idea of myself which is united in me. And it is actually the same as my mind. Now this is the procession of filiation in God. God as Father is the mind which conceives Himself. Now the picture being conceived is the Logos. Here Logos means proportion. It is the exact proportionality of Himself being just as He is. In the conception of the mind of the one God as he conceives himself perfectly.

The two images in their conception interact so much that they produce the third conception of the unification of their fields. Of the unity of the principle of coming together. And that is the third procession. We call the three processions Father, Son and Holy Ghost. But the whole thing is absolute unity. I am who I am. But different aspects of the same unity.

So that's how we explain the Trinity, which is not three separate beings. It is exactly the same being of God, being absolutely one in his Godhead. But he has the conception of the Logos. The Logos and the conceiving of the Logos have so much love of one another, so much attraction that it causes a wind: a spirit, a breath and that is what we call Holy Ghost. But we must emphasize that whenever we speak of the Trinity, it's only a sort of pictorial representation. That it is really absolutely outside our mental range. But Christ talking to people had to use some sort of terms, so the people could understand that there are three persons. By persons, we mean a personality, that is a substance that exists within itself and not something else. Colour belongs to something, but say a chair or an ash tree rests in itself. Now if there is an individual nature which rests in itself, within its own existence, we may call it a person. The second person of God is the conceived picture, which is a conceived picture and not the conceiving mind of the picture. So there is a relationship between the conceiving and being conceived. God, being what he is, the conceived mind and the conceiving of it. But the whole process is going on in the mind itself and so there is absolute unity, one with the conceiving mind, but it is in itself a different representation. And we call them different representations in order to understand in our own way the picture conceived and the conceiving mind. Now those two are in such a perfect harmony, they love each other so much that the love itself is something which unites the two. This love is not the conceiving mind or the conceived picture. That is the third person because it's something different from the other two. And so you have one nature, two processions, conception and love. You have three so-called persons and four relationships, the relationship of father to son, of son to father, of father and son to Holy Ghost and Holy Ghost to the father and son. There are four different things altogether.

That is the theology of the Holy Trinity, which is only a model of something that is beyond our conceptions. But it has some sort of analogy in our life. And I should say that in our own selves there is an analogy in our three quasi-personalities: subconscious, conscious and overconscious. And if a man talks to himself, it's not the first sign of insanity. The conscious wants to talk to the subconscious and the overconscious. Which are three different things in our own mind. And as a matter of fact talking to oneself may have a tremendous effect on George or Peter as we call the subconscious and the overconscious.

So you see there is another analogy of ourselves being created in the picture of God. It's not only that we have a field which is outside space and time and therefore covering the whole universe. The universe in its special sense is nothing in comparison to us and our field. The difference between God and us is that we cannot be focused at once throughout the entire universe while he can. Because we have to focus here on Earth or somewhere else. That is the difference between our Primary Field, and God being the field of the universe.

8

THE NAME
OF GOD[1]

Y ou ask what it is to pray "in the name" as in, "Whatsoever you
shall ask in my name, that will My Father give you".

In ancient times the *name* meant the basic proportions, basic tones, basic music. The true self. That is, to find the *name*, to know
the real name of anyone or of anything is to acquire power with that
person or thing. For example, Moses had power with God after God
had revealed to him His name, "I am who I am", and in that name he
later performed great miracles.

To pray "in the name of the Lord" is to pray in the actual proportions (set of proportions) of the Lord by tuning into the main proportions of God which are at the foundation of the whole universe. The
name given us is Word or Logos. "Word" means the primary or essential proportion present throughout the universe. In the second century
St. Justin speaks of the main proportions, as the Logos Spermatikos,
spread throughout the universe. You can find it as much in the grass
or the stones as in the air, the sea or the stars, reflecting the proportions of God Himself. The Christian is then to be the reflection of the
proportions of God.

So the name of God is everywhere—the Logos Spermatikos, and it
is for us to decipher it. We *can* find it, but it is not easy for us for we
are usually looking for it far from its essence. Our problem is generally nearby and the answer is found close to the problem itself, but we
spend our time looking for it elsewhere. In the same way the answer to

the search for the proper proportions of God is close beside us, in the signs He has given us in Creation: His Book of Life. Just as the meaning of a book lies beneath the small black signs on the printed page, the world is God's big book. But we must not stop at the outward signs. One must go deeper into it to reach its content. Then you will find the Truth. The Kingdom is around yourself, it is within yourself.[2] "You have eyes and do not see; you have ears and you do not hear, because your hearts are dull", as the Lord said in the Gospel. The answer lies beneath the surface, beneath the facts you meet in life, because life brings you not only the signs but also the answer.

We stop at the signs as physicists do today. The physicist explores nature to find its chemical composition, but utterly fails to see the meaning of it. They do not read the big book expressed quite clearly in simple speech and music, and which is all the time is in front of them. Looking at Creation, we are seeing the Logos. We are seeing the Kingdom, hearing the Kingdom but it does not convey the main content which is God because we do not see further than the outward signs. Belief usually stops at those outward signs because we put blockages against seeing the Kingdom, that other world of which Plato speaks. The physicists of today are doing exactly that. They explore nature, find out its chemical composition etc. and miss the meaning of it all through failing to read the book God has put in front of them. You have to tune in, to listen in and to look in to the Laws of Nature until you have understood what nature has to convey to you. Once you have grasped and understood it, then you can turn your mind towards organising nature so that it can, as it were, play a still better concerto. That is what we call the Will of God. You conform to the Creator who has given us human beings the power to arrange natural phenomena in such a way as to display the glorious music of the world, to praise God even more fully. He has lent us human beings the power to play on the strings of the human souls, the animal and plant souls, stones and crystals. Then if you are to fulfil the will of God, you first of all need to become a perfect resonating instrument in the great symphony of Creation.

We listen to the great Logos Spermatikos, the great music spread round the whole universe, and we understand that there are so many instruments playing their own tune. So we have to listen in to the instruments we have at hand and compose our lives within this great symphony. That is what we are doing and becoming when we believe. Then our belief is not contradictory to the Will of God. It is in perfect shape and harmony with what He wants. He has given you the instruments, and given you the decision as to what kind of music you wish to play in your own life, your surroundings and your environment. It is up to you to do it, and that is blessing. Blessing is radiating the Grace of God in such a way as to tune into the music of the universe. Whenever we can give out the Grace we have received, that Grace will make of our life an infinitely more beautiful music. The best comparison I can think of is a diver who goes down to photograph the underwater world. But it is grey-green and colourless until a strong searchlight is directed right down into it. Then there is immediately a phantasmagoria of colour and indescribable beauty. Exactly the same thing happens with the Grace of God. It is a terrific power, and it is in your hands.

9

THE

EUCHARIST[1]

The Eucharist is an aspect of marriage, of the sacrament of marriage. If you look through the Bible, you will find that God, talking through the Prophets tells Israel, "You are my wife – I am your husband." It was the only way to convey the concept of unity, of co-operation, of symbiosis between Israel and God. It's a sort of symbiosis—that is two different beings, God and Israel living together, having one life, creating a family in God and humanity, and through humanity, all of Creation. For the human being combines spirit and matter.

The whole of Creation is represented by human beings. St Paul says in Romans Chapter 8, "...the whole of Creation is in groaning and moaning expectation of the revelation of the sons of God." Therefore through us Grace should reach Creation. I ask you one question. Creation feeds you, clothes you, protects you by supplying stones for your habitations, wool for your clothes and food for eating. What do you give back to Creation? You never thought of it? No. We are the exploiters. We exploit Creation. The only thing that it asks, expects of us, is light and love. There is a tremendous love we can give to Creation. In my morning prayer or meditation I absorb the power of God , the life of God, and in evening prayer, indeed all day, I distribute that to all Creation so that through me, it can participate in the glory that is the light and love of God. Glorifying God is acknowledging his light and love. Glory means light and love, the garment of God. In Hebrew it is Shekinah, a word that is feminine. The love of God is feminine.

So you see that the relationship between God and Israel was a marriage relationship, of living together, creating a family where the person who has to extend that relationship further, to all of Creation, is Man.

Regarding the Eucharist, the bread and wine represent yourself, your problems and the problems of Creation. You offer that to God and ask Him to take it over, transform it as he did on the Cross. He took our sins. He had to die because the wages of sin is death. Once he took that into His power, into himself, he transmuted it into His Resurrection, into divine Grace, the divine glory of the Shekinah, and then He gave that back to the human being, to those who offered the same bread and the same wine. And therefore the bread and the wine, the communion, should be consecrated in the same Mass and not in the Mass before, as many priests are doing. For it is now —- here and now, that I offer my problems to Him and I ask Him to take them over, to transmute them and to give them back to me as food; the same problems but already diffused, already transmuted, resurrected. It is the mystery of the resurrection and passion.

In a marriage between two persons, exactly the same phenomenon occurs. I have my problems, my associations with my frame of mind and I give that to my wife. She takes them over. She is not at all affected by my associations. She is not affected by *my* frame of mind. She transmutes my complexes and along with her radiation she gives them back to me. And I am doing the same for her. Exactly the same happens between God and Man in the Eucharist. One of the wisest theologians told me that the Eucharist is an aspect of marriage. I did not understand it; perhaps he did not want to explain it to me then. It has taken me ten or twelve years to work it out.

Now the first aim of marriage is radiation, what Christ in the Incarnation brought about through the marriage of God and the redeemed, New Israel. The next perfect marriage was that of Our Lady and the Holy Spirit, which makes her the mother of Grace, for she is the mother of Christ. "Grace and truth came by Jesus Christ" (John Ch 1, 17).

The next aim of marriage is the mutual exchange of energy, the healing of complexes, all the blockages that prevent the flow of life in us. And therefore it produces longevity if not immortality of the marriage if properly conceived.

The third aim of marriage *if you want to*, you can have children. That explains the curse God pronounced to Eve when he said after the Fall, "I shall multiply your pains *and* your conceptions." Not *in* your conceptions as Ronald Knox translated. I have made a close analysis of the Hebrew text and the Greek text, and the Latin text, and it is definitely "and". Multiple conceptions are a curse. Women will not be able to regulate conception by the use of the mind. If you practice—shall we call it, "magical love-making", the result of it is immortality. But if it fails, it produces a child. Theologians didn't understand the principle of marriage, the curse after the Fall. It looked to them like a curse, but how could it be? Aren't we told that children are a blessing of God? Yes—but what children? First, children conceived by Grace through the sacrament of Baptism, or through the blessing of all of Creation. I mean, my life must be a constant blessing, a constant distribution of blessing to all Creation that surrounds me. We shall never stop to bring the golden rain to all of Creation. Second, I have to bring this golden rain to my wife, which in *my* case is the whole of Creation, and my Parish. Thirdly, I may conceive physical children if I want to, but that is not the essential aim of marriage. Children of Grace are essential.

The Eucharist is another aspect of the same unity because in the Eucharist you have the same unity between Man and God—that means a marriage, co-habitation, or co-living. It is not me who lives but He lives in me. That is the idea of unity between me and God, as it is only an analogical image of marriage. But marriage should conform to this unity, and not the unity conform to the human conception of marriage.

If you follow that argument, that marriage as such is an extremely sacred thing, then it appears that marriage is *the* sacrament. It is as the Eucharist, because it is the marriage between us and Christ and God.

There are two different kinds of worship of God: individual and group. You never see Christ going for his individual prayer to the church, the Synagogue. He only goes to the Synagogue for group prayer. Never for his individual prayer. For that, he always goes to the mountains. The reason for that is that from the mountains you can see wide distances. You can embrace Creation by unifying yourself with God, and immediately redistribute the power of God to Creation.

But we have completely forgotten the phenomenon of group prayer, in a church. No one has been taught, neither priest nor layman, how to operate group prayer. For a very long time we have been going to the church, listening to the Mass, where many people said the rosary or read litanies, while the Mass was said by the priest. It is exactly as if you would go to the theatre to see a performance of Shakespeare, and instead of attending to it, you were to take a novel and read it to yourself throughout the play. All that seemed to have been necessary for people attending Mass was to be physically present. They thanked God when it was over, and they could leave. That is exactly what has been happening.

Along with the new liturgical movement, the Church wants to emphasise group prayer—the phenomenon of the great drama going on, of the unity between God and Creation, of God and human beings as such—as a group and not as individuals. It is the drama in which every man in the church takes part; is an actor in the drama. Not only an onlooker; he is an actor. And the chief actor, the conductor, is the priest. Most priests and laymen know nothing about this. They just perform and say we have to offer glory to God in the sacrifice, but the idea behind it (group prayer) is practically unknown. The priest needs to know how to raise—I wouldn't say a natural spell, but a supernatural "spell" in the church. So that people coming to the church would feel "something" is going on, I don't know what, but they'd leave the Church revived, along with something that is terrific. I started a long study of it about a year and a half ago, and I have succeeded in making a "spell" in the church now. Many Protestants come to the church so as to experience it. They cry, they leave, and they say "I am a new man", but they don't know why. They experienced something in the church. I am only starting to study this, as someone in a primary school, but I'm aiming at university. There needs to be a sort of tension so that people will long to go to church. And they'll say, "What a pity it is ended" rather than "Thank God it's over. We can go away." That has been the usual psychology among Catholics. They are going to church because they have to go; they're happy when it is all over.

As the Pope has said, Christ is as much present in the Eucharist as He is present in the people gathered together for the Mass in the Church. The presence of Christ is there; that is quite right. But we never open ourselves to it.

In the church you are inside the great drama of redemption. There you have to fill yourself with these forces, and bring them back to your home, your family and to your whole environment. Wherever you are, you have to celebrate the Mass throughout the week, throughout the day; for the Mass, started at church this morning, is still going on in and with you. That means that while I am here talking to you, and you are listening, we are still, between ourselves exchanging the forces of the life of God and the sympathy of human love on which Divine Love is modulated and superimposed, and we distribute that to the walls, the furniture and everything around us.

Having opened yourself to the forces of God, you may distribute them to the plants, the little buttercups, the thistles and the birds in the leaves. Blessing is being aware of them - those particular leaves, that particular flower, seeing them as themselves, and feeling yourself in touch with them, a personal, conscious communication. You bring them the love and light you have received in your meditation, in your in-touchness with God. You can love their beauty, and tell them how beautiful they are. This conscious awareness of nature around us enriches them and us. Then try—try to feel through your skin what comes back to you. After a time you will become more sensitive, discovering the tremendous response of nature. It is not a figment of your imagination. It has been proved by scientific experiment. Take a potted plant, connect it to an electrode, amplifier and graph pen, you will find that if you are merely neutral towards it, looking at it without interest or appreciation, it will be absolutely silent (and will not flourish). But as soon as you start to love the plant, the graph needle moves; there is at once a specific response to human feelings.

An American and then a Swiss scientist have found out that plants have all the human feelings as we have of love, resentment, hatred and frustration, so it is not my imagination that when I start to love the plants, I feel their reply. There is an actual reply - the response of their field to my field; my field to the tree over there. I contact them and I give them light and love and immediately the light and love comes back to me.

Actually I was once fed by the plants. I was driving from North Wales on the way home, and I had to cover the distance to be here at a certain time. I didn't have time to stop on my way and I still had to drive an old lady to Bristol, this side of Bristol. And I was very hungry. So the very first thing I did was to give light and love to Creation all around me. I said, "Will you feed me, please? For otherwise I shall doze off with my eyes open and cause an accident". Within five minutes I was not only fed, but fizzing with energy like a bottle of champagne. I did not even want to eat for about two days. That is the reply of Creation to our request, provided we give it what it expects us to give. But we do not bother to give Creation anything. It does not even occur to us. We simply exploit nature and fail to give it anything in return. So we have to give, and then we get the reply. We are fed, and therefore need only one tenth of what we eat. Provided you love, and thus live with God, you not only live on bread but on the Word of God. This is literally true.

To return to group prayer. Priests and laymen must be trained to achieve this form of group worship in which everyone takes part. If you go to a local theatre and the performance is very poor, you are naturally annoyed and bored. But if you go to a magnificent performance of a great Shakespearean play you are absolutely delighted, and it remains with you. Now in the church, you are the actors, and the concert not only depends on the conductor—the priest—but on yourselves, how the performance is done. If you all play your part well, you should be very happy, and only longing for another performance, because you have to give out to the whole of Creation the wonderful gift of radiation you have got. If you go to Mass, fail to play your part wholeheartedly and are just bored stiff, then, of course, neither Creation benefits from you, nor from the Mass, and you have missed what you were meant to receive and to give out; to radiate to all around you.

10

DEVELOPING
FIELD AWARENESS[1]

You emit a field, and the field is present in your surrounding space. What you emit is heat in the form of infra-red radiation. The pattern, that is unique to your personality, covers the world in 1/8th of a second. You are a station transmitting your unique pattern, and if I want to tune into you, I have to tune into your pattern. I don't need to go to you to find out this and that, because your pattern covers the Earth in 1/8th of a second. So you are everywhere. My field is also everywhere. There is no distance because your pattern is here and now. What is important to know is that your thinking is in your field and not in your head, which is only a transformer. Your thinking and your self are in the field. Your body is only a transformer for your everyday life. Your consciousness.

What I am going to talk to you today is about field awareness, what it is to be aware of our field and pick up messages from our field. Actually we don't need to cover the distance from the perimeter of our field to the Earth as this will take us sixty years. We have another field, what the scientists call the Organizing Field (Primary Field), which is not of a physical nature. It is the field that organizes the molecules in a seed so that they grow into a particular shape: the shape of a human being, shape of a plant or a crystal. And it is not derived from matter, but it is above matter and beyond space and time. So it's something outside the physical world. This has been known since the early twentieth century. The German embryologist Speeman[2] started to study it.

Then other German scientists did quite a lot with it. But in their investigations, the Organizing Field was always inside the body. They didn't realize that, although they said it was outside the physical world, that it is outside space and time. So also Einstein, when he started to think about the entire space-time relationship. If you make the two connections you conclude that this field does not need to cover time and space, because it is actually present everywhere at once.

You have a daily experience of it—or perhaps weekly, when in a dream, you may see something that later comes to pass. Or you see a place, that ten years later you come upon, and you know you have been there before. You simply picked up the signals from your Secondary Field. But due to the fact that you have a primary field present, regulating, modulating or even directing the Secondary Field, the message comes through to your Primary Field, that we call the Soul.

I want you to be aware of those two, different fields—The Primary Field that provides the organization of the whole body. We call it the Soul, the soul of a plant or a crystal, outside the material world. And the Secondary Field: we emit heat, sound, the sound and the heat from our functioning organs. But it is under the influence of our Primary Field. Also of our emotions.

If I am angry then this anger, this emotion arises from a certain set of beliefs that a danger is coming to me, so I need to counter this anger. This set of beliefs which is primarily a spiritual thing, will affect my emotions. Those emotions produce bloodshot eyes, opening of capillary vessels, rosy cheeks, clenching teeth. This is reflected in the Secondary Field. But the Primary can pick up immediately what is happening in the Secondary, even if the Secondary is 60 light years away from us. Because the Primary is present everywhere.

Now that we have grasped the idea of this field, I would like to expand a little on the subject. The Primary Field is present outside space, covering the whole universe. But the Secondary field travels with the speed of light and covers a tremendous space, with a huge perimeter because it expands not in one direction but in every direction. So, if you are sixty years old, your field covers one hundred and twenty light years. You are a giant in comparison to the body. But we have done everything possible to limit ourselves to the body. And we exclude from our awareness and from our consciousness, that we may be aware of our field and pick up messages from it. Those people who have some sort of awareness of it by accident, may be aware of what is going on in the next room. We call that ability clairvoyance. They may be aware of what happened thirty years ago, or two thousand years ago. They see for example events in Palestine during Christ's time. Catherine Emmerich. knew Palestine thoroughly, the stones, fires, though during her life she never left her village near Cologne in Germany. But all her descriptions of the Palestine geography and the way that people lived two thousand years ago fit exactly with the knowledge of the archaeologists and geographers. So obviously, she had been there; and we ask how? Very simply she picked up the messages from those days because her Primary Field, outside space and time, covered over a thousand years backward and a thousand years forward in time.

Imagination is our power to focus here, there or anywhere in our field. And it's not the same as fantasy. Fantasy is something which I spin out of my own construction. Imagination is something that reconstructs the actual facts. Now usually the two are very much mixed together and we don't know imagination from fantasy. Because we never try to be field aware. This field awareness is possible to achieve in some way or other, if you have the time and technique. But if we are field aware, then if we focus our imagination, and not fantasy, on New York we'll see cars going up and down and people walking about. But for that you have to separate imagination from fantasy. And that is a big task; to know how to do it. Because you might say, I'm imagining that, but actually I'm fantasising it. So that is not field awareness. That is awareness of my own construction.

Now field awareness must lead us to imagination as such, the power to construct messages from often very weak signals coming to us from outside, because the field in New York is very weak. You must realize that it is extremely important to develop field awareness. And that's where clairvoyance comes in and clairaudience, and seeing past times and seeing future times.

We have to gradually drop ourselves down into our imagination, into our awareness, our consciousness that we have such a field. That you extend over the Earthly globe and over the starry space. Once you have grasped the idea, then you start to produce field awareness. That means trying to put your attention, focusing your attention to what is coming toward you. And obviously you will not use your two external eyes but your internal eyes that you use every day in your dreams. You may say, that is only a figment of my fantasy. Not necessarily. Because very often in a dream you see reality that later comes to pass. How did you see it? With your eyes when you were sleeping in a bed? Obviously not.

There is a centre in your brain that picks up the messages from outside. Once you pick up messages from outside and start to transform them into pictorial waves or auditory waves, or tactile waves, or any other sensory waves, then you start to develop your field awareness. Indeed you will know that you have a field, that you have to be aware of this field, of messages coming to you, then you will start to use more and more of your brain as a transformer. Up until now only one millionth of a millionth of your brain is used. The rest is sitting quietly, as it has been for I don't know how many centuries, without any use at all. As you pick up those messages from outside, you will start to wake up. The point is that now, you still get those messages but you have blocked yourself against any messages coming to you from below.

So we have to open the wall between our subconscious mind. That means from our field. The two triangles (Figure 3-A) represent the human being, my ego, my conscious side, my individual subconscious—for instance that twenty years ago I was in Piccadilly Circus and saw some men walking there. And that was registered somewhere in my brain. And if some doctor were to put some electrodes on my brain and supply an impulse, I could see all that again. That is my individual subconscious. It has nothing to do with any of you. It resides in my brain. If you get a strong impulse, you play it through your memory, as long as you *can* remember it. But if you have lost the way to that particular jumble in your brain, then you are not able to find your way to that particular cell and you don't remember. If you go over the event several times, then a path is made and you can remember it.

That is your individual subconscious. And now we come to your collective subconscious which is tribe, nation, human race, animal, vegetable, mineral and energy as such. It's not nicely made up like that, but for the sake of understanding things, it has been divided into those classes. Now it is collective which means it's the same for everybody. Like grass it grows from a common ground. So the field of all of Creation is common to all of us. I can dip into this field and know about everything that is there. Take a little stone step in Mrs. Smith's house. If I tune into the field of the step I can know exactly how the step was made, when and how, when the stone was formed millions of years ago, where it was situated, everything about the stone. So you see that the messages can refer not only to family but to minerals and to energy as such. For example, Bruce MacManaway works with energy. We may tune into the field of energy, and then we get the energy. As for the art of tuning in, we never learned it because we didn't know such things exist. So when you don't know, you don't start. You don't start so you don't get it. If you don't know that you can write, you never start to write. People once didn't know that you can put some ideas into matter, so they never started to make letters. And then somebody invented the hieroglyphs, and other letters, and then gradually we could put down letters, and now we have the art of putting ideas onto paper. A terrific idea. You don't realize what a great invention it was.

To make you aware of this, I'm going to tell you a story. Back in the fourth century there was a man who wanted to find the Kingdom of God. He goes around and he asks priests about the Kingdom of God. He can't find any answer. Eventually someone tells him that there is a very wise man living in the desert in Egypt. So being a rich man he goes there as he is directed and comes past the desert, to a beautiful green place. He comes to this place, and finds an old man there, blue eyes and grey hair. The man looks at the visitor and says, "What are you doing my son?" He says, "I heard about you and I came to ask about the Kingdom of God." "Maybe you will be able to understand that. Sit down. Stay with me. After three days perhaps I shall be able to tell you something about it." So he stays. And the old man never says a word to him. He follows the old man wherever he goes. The old man is in perfect harmony with his surroundings. A beautiful serene something is there. Animals come to drink the water, and he greets them, lions, hyenas and so on. There is this gentle power in the trees, the animals, the water. He suspects that there is a sort of communication between the old man and the others. After three days they go to a rock, the place they usually go in the evening for a sort of contemplation of the beauty. There's a lovely feeling. The sunshine has just started to turn red. The gentleman cannot stand it any more and turns to the old man and asks him to tell him about the Kingdom of Heaven. The old man says, "I think you are ready for that. See what is written here in the sand. The visitor sees Greek letters, and so he starts to read, 'In the beginning was the Word, and the Word was with God.' The old man says, "Now you can read. Before you could not see anything but clear sand, but because you can now see the words in the clear sand, I can talk to you."

And strange enough the Greeks said that Ideas can be formed into words. And you can describe them, see the history of ancient times, the lovely cosmos of people, the speech of ancient people, beautiful places. Anything can be put into those words. If you were newly born today, and you would see the beauty around you, what would you say? "I can't understand all this. I can see all sorts of beautiful things but I can't make sense of them." You would see all sorts of science ideas and find them funny. But if you could read the total beauty around you, it would be different. The difference between this world and that is exactly the same as the difference between the content of God and the big book of nature surrounding you. But you don't know how to read it. You take it for granted but you don't know what to make of it. The beauty around you has a terrific content, much bigger than you imagine and which will lead you to the Kingdom. A symbolic representation. Let it be symbolic. And the difference between them is exactly the same as the difference between the beauty of the world and the beauty of the Kingdom.

Well, that's the idea of how we take for granted different things and we don't see and we don't read. We hear and we don't understand, Christ said, because our hearts are greedy. What does that mean? We are closed and we don't accept the signal coming to us from the surroundings. That means from the field.

Obviously distant matter imposes itself on your eye and you start to feel the little field inside yourself in order to promote certain ideas. You may be clever enough to see that this is an F an A, M,I, L, and a Y. You connect those letters and form the idea of "Family"— the people of the family. You see the gathering of the family and strange enough you may be able to tune into the individual field of the family. Then you may sense in this family or that family, things that are not very pleasant, but you don't know what they are. You don't know because you haven't trained yourself to pick up messages from the field.

Now you may have some idea of what field awareness means: picking up signals from the surrounding field. It happens very often when you sit in your room and somebody comes in. And you have the first impression, that there's something peculiar coming in. Not just about the shape of the body but something of the personality. And you are moved. You smile, you breathe deep, bringing in the messages of the field. And this sort of tuning into the field has to be a constant experience in our lives. You can tune into the field and remember what these letters are. Symbols of some ideas behind them. So also the shape of the body, the look of your eyes, the sound of your voice, and so on, are symbols that convey something much deeper, something of the field.

Now this is one practical device in order to make you aware how you can start to feel the field. You may have done it in your childhood but never realized it in that way. Perhaps you did but someone killed that sensitivity with a single word.

84

How can you feel and be aware of your field? You must remember the rule in psychology, "How we see ourselves thus we become." It's a rule in psychology and in everyday life. It means, if you want to see yourself as a housewife, or an engineer or an architect, or something else, you will enter a different psychic state and eventually, if you have the 3-Ps, persistence, perseverance and patience you will eventually achieve your goal. If you have negative thinking you may put a blockage against your goal, but if you are a positive thinker you will always achieve what you want to be. If you want to be a physicist you will look into physics books, notice all sorts of physical things and eventually you will become a physicist, a Rutherford or Einstein or whatever because you see it in your mind.

So if we want to perceive or to be sensitive to our field, we have to pick up signals. We have to see our field. And that is very important. Now we don't want to see only our field. We also want to see the field of God. God is not an old gentleman sitting on a chair, with a beard, and looking at how beautiful everything is. He is a field surrounding ourselves, penetrating ourselves.

There are two processions, the procession of the Son if you want to call it so, and the procession of love. There are three persons, different aspects of the same thing, and there are four relationships: the conceiving mind to the conceived picture, the conceived picture to the conceiving mind, the love of the mind to the conceived picture, and the love of the conceived picture to the mind. And we call it 1-2-3-4. One nature, two processions, three persons and four relations. Relation means some sort of musical proportionalities, the proportions reflecting the supreme mind of God. Its Logos.

Through Logos, that means through the pictorial representation of God, the mind of God brought the outside world into existence. Obviously the power is not the will which is love between the mind and the conceived picture, but it is the imagination which brought forth the world. The imagination is the power; not will power. The visualization, picture-making. How we see, thus we become. And we project it, put it forth as the Hindus would call it. There is a sort of creation myth, for everything in our life boils down to the imagination, the construction of the right thing.

If you use imagination in a positive way, if you want to heal somebody, you have to see, for example – the cancer. You don't see it developing because you stop it by this picture-forming. In actual healing you see the shrinking cancer and the development of life. And through that thought which imprints itself on every biological cell, the cell gradually develops into the picture that you have in mind. And here you have the ultimate mechanism of how healing takes place. It's always the function of your imagination. Not fantasy. But if you put fantasy into it, you can produce something like fireworks, a fire you need to put out. That is fantasy as opposed to your actual imagination.

Therefore you want to be aware of the field—the overconscious part, that means the field of God. The field of the supreme, the field that is conscious everywhere. But He created a world that is not a perfect world. He wanted the world to achieve perfection by progressing. And this progression must be done by Man, who through the imagination can lead the world toward perfection; by sensing the field and having exactly the idea of how to proceed in order to get there.

And Man spoiled all of this, because He cut himself off from the light. He was in Paradise having the full light on himself, and he was star gazing. This light of God descended completely and invaded the whole of the collective subconscious, that means the whole of Creation. He, representing symbolically the whole of Creation was master of it, could direct it. But he said, "No, I want to investigate that without you. Free of the knowledge of good and evil." So the light went out; he was separated from it by the ego. "I want to do it myself," or as a child says, "I need it for myself mummy!" He wanted to proceed, starting with himself. In exactly the same way the man behaves like a child in its primal state.

Though he said, "No" to the light of God, he was still the master who had to lead the world toward perfection, but he lost his way. So he started to go there, there and there. He did not know where to go because there was no light. The light of God. And because the light is gone, you cannot love someone you don't know. You may say, "I would want to love something but I don't know what it is." You might pick up something in the collective subconscious and long to love it. But you can't love whatever is not conscious within you.

So was lost the love of Creation; the ability to identify myself with the object. Because when I love a woman I tend to identify myself with the woman. I want to be close to the woman. Or try to be close to the plant I love. The direction of my love is from me toward the object. I have the mental ability to tune into her field, and then I'm identified with her. But once I lost the ability to tune in because I lost the knowledge of the field, I didn't know how to direct love. I couldn't pick up the signal from plants, animals or stones. I didn't know what the goal is. I lost the ability to contact the field, the collective field and so I started to go in different directions.

Perhaps a representation of this state is much of modern music; they go at it but can't find the road. But the music also can be an expression of something in the subconscious mind that wants to find a way. That means, there's something awakening in the youngster who plays it. Something restless. He wants to find something which he can't find because he doesn't know where to look. There's no light or leadership. And because of this lack of leadership, of direction, Creation didn't go towards the Christ goal, but went here, and here, and there like modern music.

Perfection needs to be achieved by men, who need a master, a representative of all Creation, spiritual and physical. Because we are the unique creation which has both elements. Therefore the Incarnation could only be in Man who combines the two: the collective subconscious and the collective overconscious.

If I tune into my field of the higher strata of myself, the High Self, I see myself in radiation going out with millions of rays. You sometimes see the sun reflected in a piece of glass, where you feel millions of rays going out. Now, see your field like that, going out in all directions and you start to realize that it's me, this field. Not my radiation but me. And when I think, the radiation changes. Later on when you start to be aware of this, you'll see that the radiation changes rapidly. And its colours. You'll see in the radiation of the sun different colours, all the colours of the rainbow. All the harmonics are there corresponding to your thoughts and moods. You start to be aware of the field but not yet aware of the messages in the field. And then you realize that this field is penetrating another field. Instead of working in your lower field, you start to accommodate to the higher field. And explore.

Figure 11: Andrew Glazewski with Sir George Trevelyan
at Attingham Park

Figure 12: Andrew Glazewski circa 1945 in uniform

Figure 13: Andrew speaking with parish children.
Isles of Scilly mid 1960s.

Figure 14: Evening talk on St Marys, Isles of Scilly.
L-R Andrew Glazewski, Ludi How, Paul Kieniewicz 1972

11

WHAT HAPPENS WHEN WE DIE?[1]

Now in connection with the field, obviously when the man drops his body, in what we call death, he doesn't drop his field. Because the field is part of him, but not part of the body. Therefore, the Primary Field still exists in the physical. The Secondary Field doesn't develop any more. Now I think you can call the Primary Field the soul. By the word soul, we mean the principle of unity in plants, animals or human beings. Now the human soul performs the functions of the vegetable life, the animal life and the mental life. Obviously as regards plant and animal life there are different degrees, different varieties of soul. After death the human field, or human soul performs a different function, on different levels, mental and spiritual. We can call it mental or spiritual but the name is irrelevant. The function of it is what is important. So I think that if we go on, studying the fields we will find that in the Primary Field there are all sorts of levels which I don't think can be proved physically. Except by our experience in developing degrees of consciousness I should say. Or levels of consciousness. There is the consciousness of our six sense perceptions which are of the material world. Along with the consciousness of our normal field we become conscious of the mental world, and then the world of proportions and then those different proportions that divide into different keys, and then to different compositions.

So from your experience in the material, mental or emotional, we can find that there is in us a tremendous possibility for developing all sorts of higher levels which are very different from one another: an expansion of consciousness such as described by Steiner that we have hardly developed. Therefore we say that we are only using only a millionth of our brain, referring also to our consciousness. We achieve it through our brain, by field awareness which I call the seventh sense. Developing field awareness is one of the tasks which we have to exercise as much as we can.

Perhaps it would be relevant to say that the soul, as in the Primary Field itself, is a closed physical system. A closed physical system means, that if I put my leg in a bracket, and then push against it to try to lift myself, I'm not able to do it because the more I lift, or press upward, the more the leg presses downward. An open physical system is where I have outside my system, something like a lever that I can push against and so lift myself. After death the soul is similar to a closed physical system in that, once the soul is left to herself, she can no longer refer to the body. While alive it can refer to the body and the body to the soul.

Here you see the importance of the knowledge of angelic beings. They are closed physical systems in that they are not capable of moving from one level to another. They are bound to their own level. While we are surrounded by the body we can develop, go from one level to another.[2]

The evil spirits are also closed physical systems. That doesn't mean that they cannot go back and say I'm sorry for what I've done. That very moment they would be accepted back again, into what they call heaven. But the harmony of his will is the evil spirit's nature. Back in the Garden of Eden he said, "I will not serve," because all of nature had evolved to the next key; the next key of the relationship. Say we were created in C major, and then the whole evolution went into C sharp minor. And he said, "No, I want to stay in C major because in C major, I being of C major, was first. In C sharp minor I am not the first; I am not the leader in the big orchestra. I prefer to stay where I am." And the Good Lord says, "All right. If you prefer where you are, you'll stay there. The nature of it is that you're stuck in the key where you've chosen to be." And therefore he is in constant disharmony and constant contradiction because his whole nature craves for him to be in C sharp minor but he says "No, I am here where I am."

Therefore he cannot by himself get out of this closed system because his nature is such that he cannot refer to his nature. He doesn't want to because his nature is against his will. But if somebody comes from outside, that outside help may do something for him.

Try to compare that with variable stars. There are two types of stars in the heavens, nova stars and dwarf stars. But there are also stars which are pulsating. These are called usually Cepheids, changing in times of, from a few days to some hours, of our time here on Earth. Within six hours a star can vary from the size of our sun to twice the size of our sun in space, and then back to the size of our sun. This is obviously a pulsating star. Now sometimes a pulsating star will explode. I imagine that it's a sort of atomic explosion on an astronomical scale. And then that star becomes a bright star for about six months and then it vanishes. This is in all probability because the forces keeping the star together can no longer contain it and so the star explodes. But there are also dwarf stars. Instead of exploding those stars collapse. We have an example of such a star with the companion of the star, Sirius. Sirius is known to have an orbiting star that is invisible[3]. It has collapsed so that it doesn't emit much light. Astronomers say that one cubic inch of this star's matter will weigh about two tons. The magnetic field of this star is about two million gauss, compared to the magnetic field of the Earth which is 0.63 gauss. The difference in the magnetic fields raises the question, why?

Now you have those two types of stars, the nova and the dwarf star. One encloses matter in a terrific pressure, and the other is expanding. And you have here the picture of two different laws: The law of self and contempt of God and the law of God and contempt of self. Saint Augustine wrote about it. Selfishness can represent the magnetic field of the dwarf star. The nova star, the exploding star, represents the expansion of consciousness where we are starting to be conscious, a growing awareness of the field of the whole universe and of different levels there. So both stars are analogous to the state of the soul in heaven and hell; in the bondage of self-love, or a complete expansion throughout the vast universe of mind, where we are conscious of the universal consciousness, which is understanding and love and which we call God, who is aware of Himself. So we speak of a personal God not in the sense that He is a person as we are, or has a body, but that He has a personal field. Which means, conscious of His love, and His understanding, and having some basic relationship in Himself and with us. There is one God and two processions, three persons and four relationships.

Now I've covered the analogy of the nova star and dwarf star. We pass onto field awareness and self awareness. And this self awareness, the selfish love is a perfect representation of a closed physical system. Now I suppose that the collapsed angels which are similar to collapsed stars, or dwarf stars, are in themselves eternally condemned to this state, but if someone comes from the outside and cuts the lines of force of the magnetic field, then they will immediately expand and explode. That means that if somebody can change their will, they will immediately be accepted back again into heaven.

12

THE PRACTICE
OF GROUP HEALING[1]

A G: The first basic psychological rule is how you see yourself,
thus you become. What is very important is visualization.
If you visualize yourself as a small entity in your body, then
of course the surface and the spaces are very small. But if you visualize yourself as covering a diameter of a hundred light years, because your field has gone in every direction with the speed of light;
you're fifty one, and your field covers 102 light years diameter, and if
you fill all these spaces at once with Light-Love Technique, and also
fill your Organizing Field which is above matter, and beyond time
and space, it makes a fantastic conduit. The healing power will also
have to have the same visualization, because as far as I see it, healing is to a very large extent the result of your visualization. And you
want to heal. So if you cure only the body, the field will still contradict you, because the field is partly a function of the body, and the
body is partly a function of the field. And so the illness will persist;
remain in the field.

MacManaway: Because the condition returns?

AG: Yes. But if you cure both, then there's no return. And vast spaces
are covered, the surface is so big. The impact on the body is absolutely
like an atomic explosion of an astronomical size. You follow?

MacManaway: I do indeed. The key seems to me as far as I'm concerned, is that healing covers the space.

AG: Yes. field awareness as I call it.

MacManaway: The Field Awareness is inevitable because you can't help it. You don't have to think about it. It's something that happens because you are.

AG: You draw your attention to your field, and therefore you start to develop your awareness of this field.

MacManaway: It's a form of the field filled with positive thought. Because this field whose existence we accept, has got to be correlated with the fact which, biblically and otherwise we recognize, can be penetrated by an adverse influence. What if the field is filled with positive thought, through an exhaling impulse? Is this the key?

AG: Yes. In other words, like with an organism, you have an invader who tries to invade your body and force his own vibration into the body, and prevent the body's healing vibration to act. So also there's an invader in your field which wants to prevent your own field from vibrating to your pattern, and impose its own pattern. So expelling means reinforcing your own positive vibration. Therefore positive thinking is so important. The visualization of your positive thinking is not in your head but in the whole field. I'm quite sure that if you develop this awareness of the field, the power is simply fantastic. In no comparison to the body. I recently saw it. I knew that I could shut the whole earthly globe by an act of will. It was terrifying. And there it is. Bang, and nothing exists. And I knew that I could do it. I had to make sure and I withdrew. I was afraid of it. And it never came back.

MacManaway: Never came back?

AG: Never came back. I was in church and I realized that all those people are there, and I could do something. It could scare them to death. But I knew that it could happen. Bang—Squeezed to nothing. It was a terrifying thought.

MacManaway: Tremendous power.

AG: That's what I call power. I forced this thing to obey. I wanted to end it. Done.

MacManaway: Andrew, two points as an individual who is trying to evolve, become a channel, and as a member of a group, the leader of a group. The question of techniques arises. You are suggesting that one replaces the limited protective screen by such a positive expanding power that nothing can penetrate it. Accepted. The question of technique arises. How do we practice it? Is this covered in your phrase, Love-Light Technique?

AG: Oh I think so. It's only a question on how to visualize it.

MacManaway: Can you please expand on that.

AG: The Love-Light Technique as I saw it for a very long time involved linking myself with the body and pushing the light and love outward.

MacManaway: And the levels of consciousness of which you are aware, physical, and mental?

AG: But it's still relative to the body. Here I am limited by the perimeter of the body. But gradually as an awareness of the field started to grow, I understood that I have to fill not only the body. The whole field must be filled with love and light. I should be a huge flame of astronomical, galactic size, of fire, of understanding and light. And I have to visualize myself as opening, not here, but opening vast spaces of astronomy, astronomical connections. Love and light in every way. Everything in you, the body which is somehow a function of this field. And if I don't fill the body, there will still be still something not covered by this love and light. And negative darkness can attach itself to the body and the radiation too, which I have to throw off. Therefore I have to fill this field, and the spaces and the body. The speed with which you start to go, with your psychic realizations, is tremendous. It's been three weeks since I started that.

MacManaway: Andrew, this is very exciting. As recently as that?

AG: Yes, since we met. And of course before that, I had this idea that the thinking takes place in the field. It is an education. I still think that for me it's an education.

MacManaway: This whole notion that you think in the field and transfer to the body what you are aware of?

AG: The implications. We still don't see them. But I have been told that that is the solution. You have to transfer your realization to the field and not to the body. And here is the solution to the problem of understanding, and putting everybody into the field of love, of understanding and the love of God. From the emptiness in the world to the fullness of God's realization. And I'd say, since you left, this gradually started to increase in me, the light and love. And suddenly it started to go wild. And the more you go the faster the speed acquired. More and more strength.

MacManaway: Andrew, may I question you about this. You say that in our group work, instead of establishing a protective screen, to use a military phrase, we visualize an expanded consciousness in terms of the field; the field of which our bodies and other levels of consciousness of which we are unconscious, are simply transformers at a lower level. Seeing the vastness of the field, we set about filling that field with such a positive Christ force that nothing could penetrate it, and therefore protection doesn't enter in. Could you expand on this because two questions immediately occur? How do we put this into words? What picture are we to create in the minds of a group? Patricia and I are sitting now in our room. We can see this. We spent a number of years studying these things. So for us this particular visualization is not difficult. Both of us can see the discipline, the transformer at the centre of a vast field. But as to a technique for putting this into play in a group, or perhaps in a group at this stage?

AG: I don't know. How far is the group aware of this? Is prepared?

MacManaway: For us this is tremendously thrilling. The thought that one can overcome the problem of psychic and spiritual attack in this way is tremendous.

AG: I think that we have to start with the idea that God is nearer to us than we are to ourselves. That He is within us. The Kingdom of God is within you.

MacManaway: So how to release it?

AG: How to release Him? That means opening ourselves. Now to open ourselves we should not limit ourselves to the body. The body and the field are wherever we are. The radiation. His expansion in us in a sense. So we are actually subdued to His will and His love, understanding and light. Now that will probably create certain pictures in the group. The group will then ask the question, for a further elucidation of this picture. And then we'll say how we see it. This one will see one way. Someone else will see a different way. So it's up to us then to realize what we have to deal with in the group and how we have to expand this idea into individuals of the group, in order that there is a certain unified field of understanding in the group. As a group field. You follow?

MacManaway: Only in theory. There is a high degree of seeing required of a group leader. You have to be very aware of those who are at odds.

AG: No doubt about it. But I think that is a matter for discussion in the group which is already introduced into this sort of way of thinking. And individuals will immediately raise objections, questions or insinuations. How they thought, what they think of it. Then it's up to the leader to smooth it out, to unify conceptions. And then leaders of particular groups should meet and discuss these unification issues.

MacManaway: The technique to doing this will take some illustrating. The realization of Christ within is a key point.

AG: A key point. Christ as supreme Logos, supreme proportions, supreme light.

MacManaway: As supreme light. I can sit here and agree with you. But how? How do we go about it?

AG: We can't do with simple love. We have to realize that Christ is within us. The Kingdom of God is within you. Now the picture of the Kingdom of God is a picture of tremendous love and light and joy. Peace, serenity. Hence we have to develop first of all the awareness of tremendous love and life against which we have put up all the shutters. So as we open our shutters within us, we realize the point which is the centre of the field, and that is the body.

MacManaway: So let me say back again. We realize that …

AG: That the light within us must be in the centre of the field, and that is in the body. And then as I see it, the Kingdom is not only within me but goes out in all ways. So I suddenly open myself not only here in the centre of my body, but I open myself in my consciousness, which is covering the whole field with light and love. And this consciousness gradually will expand from the surrounding narrow ring to astronomical spaces, to the moon and further up, going on and on. But I think we have to start from the centre and move outside rather than from outside going toward the centre. What do you think now? Do you see that or not?

MacManaway: Yes, I see it Andrew as an intellectual exercise, that the light is within and that we are in its stream, that surrounds us. If we can accept it intellectually, or much more than intellectually. If we can accept that this indeed happens…

AG: Grasp it and also experience it.

MacManaway: In the experiencing of it, and the release without reservation. This is an act of faith.

AG: In a way yes.

MacManaway: Laying yourself open. You've got to be persuaded that in laying yourself open that there's a Christ expansion that fills everything so positively that all negative thoughts can have no possible domination.

AG: Yes.

MacManaway: I become a menace. ….

AG: The even distribution of the forces is realized.

MacManaway: It's fine to say. But as a technique, how? This is presumably summed up in your Love-Light Technique.

AG: I'll tell you how I see it. I see it like sand on the beach which has heat here and heat there. And we spread the field evenly with light and love.

MacManaway: With light and love. We'll come back to this light and love in a minute. Now as a technique...

AG: As a technique, I see the light progresses into the field farther and farther.

MacManaway: From within.

AG: From within. And the impact becomes so strong that it smoothes the field completely of all the blockages, blocks and little stones, and unevenness in the field, knots here and there, all disappearing completely. A vast space of smooth light and love. In flames.

MacManaway: Released through the heart. In love. So we've got to bring in the Buddha to understand, through the intellectual level.

AG: What do you mean by the Buddha?

MacManaway: Well the light; of the heart.

AG: The light, yes. For me Buddha is a man. Not God. I believe in God's light.

MacManaway: All right. For me God overrides the lot. The Buddha influences enlightenment. The Buddha taught light. Enlightenment. And Jesus taught love.

AG: Well Jesus taught light and love. Buddha was a teacher. We have to bring in the light of God as Logos; as the son of God.

MacManaway: So if we raise the love of God; the light. What's a better word as enlightenment won't do? Understanding or am I mixing metaphors? We have to fuse these two things the light and the love.

AG: For me, love is the Holy Ghost. Well that's at least how it works in the Trinity. What we can say is only a sort of vague representation in words, because we can't conceive it completely. The conceiving picture of God Himself is the reality. A reality which is absolutely united with the mind. There is one unity in humans, and that is in Nature, but it's a light. And he is the light of God. This understanding as I call it is the light of understanding. And when we understand, we love what we understand. It's the fire. That's what the Holy Ghost means. Now any teacher below may teach it, but he is not this light and this love. So I would say that this conception of the Trinity is far above the ordinary mind of the people in the group.

If you talk to the group then they won't grasp it. If you first fill yourself and then the group with the feeling that we are opening the shutters to the light and understanding, then they will understand something. So you open the shutters to light and understanding. And the more you open them, the more the penny will drop by repetition. And then you see that this understanding of light is also conceived as tremendous love. And we can do that. But we have to first cut hesitation from it. For you see yourself as understanding, and this understanding covers vast spaces of the universe. And this brings the fire of love. The fire spreads farther and farther down to the ground. High up in the air, it covers the globe and it goes to the moon and sun, planets and then the next star and next star, father and farther.

That is a representation of a picture. If they repeat it, then they will start to understand in their own way; because they open themselves. And that picture will eventually change from light to perfect understanding. They will just grasp it then. Be aware of it. But before you see you have to open yourself to the light, you have to see the light of God: to see the fire, to look and believe it. And gradually the whole thing progresses and as it progresses, the light and love will be far away, in the far distances of the field, but at the centre of the field there will be already the understanding of the heart. I understand here and then there and then there, and further, according to how I have seen. But I think if we keep in mind the law of psychology—how you see, thus you become, then you have to create a visual picture of it, of light and love and understanding. And let the rest be governed by God himself. God will do the rest.

Which reminds me, I have one point of view and you have another point of view. But when we come together we start to work in a square power, a power of ten. Because everyone brings a different picture, and some we got by revelation. A flash of light will give you a completely different conception on how to do the whole thing. So you have to go through the door that way, with a picture to begin with, to open to the light. The light awakens, and then we realize that our field covers the earth's globe, and then goes on into the vast space, on and on. And with this light comes the fire. The light lights the fire, the love starts to glow and embrace everything. Whatever you meet in the world.

MacManaway: Tremendously exciting.

AG: Fantastic. And that's only the normal mind. The ordinary physical world. And then you gradually go to the next stage, the next level. It's beyond any expression. The next stage will be to look upon the world and on yourself as a body. From the distances of the perimeter of the field you see the small body. Let's take it from here and put it there. You focus yourself on the body, take it from here to there, and there you are. As a technique of transport. You follow?

Maybe that's enough for now. You have to sleep on it. And once you sleep on it you can later on say, "This fits with my ideas and this doesn't."

Because I'm not definitely sure that all of this picture is right. Somehow I see it but I'm not sure how I see it. I haven't got a clue.

13

THE
HEALING HAND[1]

S ince the time of Christ, claims have been made repeatedly of the possibility of healing ailments by the hand. Can such persistent claims be without foundation? Is there any scientific rationale for them? There is no doubt that in very many cases such healings actually took place. Were they due to mere suggestion, or are there any possible scientific explanations for such facts?

To the writer, who apart from being a physicist and scientist, is primarily a theologian, it is quite obvious that in accordance with the theological principle that "Grace never contradicts nature but builds upon it," (and this applies to miracles as well), there must be a certain hidden and unknown physical law behind such healing hands. What could this law be?

Long studies, pursued in different universities of the Continent for eleven years, in different branches of knowledge, provided a sufficient basis to start an independent but methodical research into the healing phenomenon. After a preliminary study of how the so called healers approached the problem, it became evident that any claims that some sort of magnetism is at work had to be dismissed. Such claims could not be substantiated. The existence of electromagnetic waves in the infra-red band is obvious, for the very simple reason that heat (infra-red radiation) surrounds the body. The same applies to the sound field. A very faint noise surrounds the body producing a sonic field. This field is actually a function of the gross body metabolism. Despite the presence of the sonic and thermal fields, it became more and more evident that the static electrical field associated with the human body was a prominent factor.

It was shown by the writer in his paper, "The Gravitational Wave"[2], that sound and static electrical fields are intimately connected.

Very many healers have claimed that they can sense in their hands, at certain definite distances around the body, a faint prickling, heaviness, coolness, etc. As a matter of fact the writer can sense it too. The writer has also found that practically anybody can be trained to sense such disturbances, but because of the very faintness of the phenomena, they have escaped our notice. However, could those disturbances only be a feature of the imagination or even hallucinations, for how could they be explained in terms of modern physics? What are they? It is enough to look through the papers of the above mentioned Proceedings[2], to see just how much research has been done by various people in this field.

After a thorough study of electro-physiology by the author of the works of the physicist and biologist J.C Bose[3], it was obvious that electrical charges play a prominent part in the functioning of any kind of organism. The very basis of metabolism is electrolysis. The electrical properties of biological cells exert a potential difference usually of many millivolts in magnitude, though sometimes two volts of potential may occur between the nucleus and the membranes[4]. It is known also that in some cases the potential difference between two points on the skin of humans rises up to 14,000 volts, though normally it amounts to a few hundred. The crackling shirt when removed shows the existence of such a static field. Hence, there is no doubt that there must be an electrostatic field around the body. Such a field must be at least to a certain extent the function of the electrostatic field of the respective organs of the body, as the intensity of this field differs between different parts of the body. All electrocardiograms and encephalograms are based on such potential differences.

It is also clear, that the electrical state of the air surrounding the body, its humidity, its temperature, exerts an effect upon this very field. Such a field must have a relationship with the body organs. A simple disturbance of the rH or pH in a respective area or organ of the body has an immediate influence on this field. Hence, the field should show the small differences in the functioning of such organs. Likewise, the reverse should be true, that the field should influence the functioning of the biological cells[5]. Let us take a simplified example: suppose that the liver is disturbed in its functions. As a result the balance of electrical charges is upset, becoming more positive, and in the surrounding air negative charges are attracted to the vicinity of the liver. The negative charge in the surrounding air attracts the positive charge in the liver. Now, speaking electrically, not chemically, the circulatory system has, among other functions, the function to restore the electrical balance of the organism. However, in the above example, it may not have enough absorbing force to neutralize the surplus charges from the liver, because those are retained locally in the liver by the negative charges in the air.

Now, if the hand is introduced into such a field, this hand acts as a capacitor or a sort of condenser, the charges in the air will be absorbed by such a capacitor. When hand is then withdrawn, some of the excess negative charge in the air field will have been removed. As a result of this action of decreasing the strength of the air field, the circulatory system will have enough absorbing force to reabsorb the surplus of positive charges from the liver, restoring its former electrical state in a short period of time. Naturally, just one introduction of the hand will not be sufficient to neutralize the air field; but if it is introduced many times, complete neutralization will be achieved and the former, normal state of the organ is restored. A useful comparison may be made to emptying a barrel of water with a glass. The glass must be dipped into the water until it is full (or adsorbing charges onto the hand); the water emptied and the glass filled again (or rubbing off the excess charges and placing the hand in the field again). Such a series of actions will have to be repeated many times before the barrel is emptied (or the field cleared). This example is purposely simplified in order to demonstrate the underlying mechanism. Needless to say, the actual problems involved are far more complicated, but for lack of space a more detailed explanation is omitted.

Anyway, the approach of this article is purely an electrical one. I have no intention of ignoring the importance of the chemical aspects, though for the sake of space I must pass them by. The human body has been compared to a complicated electrical network. Hence, certain general rules true of such a network should also be true of the human body. It is known that if in a complicated electrical network a resistor breaks down somewhere, then by Kirchov's law, a high voltage will appear in other places. In high voltage transmission lines this results in a brush discharge and a leakage of electricity, thanks to the much higher voltage. This is precisely what happens in the human body. In a disturbed organ, thanks to hyperthermia, or other reasons, the normal resistance breaks down, with the result that in other respective points a higher voltage appears. It is known that in some Chinese Acupuncture Points a higher voltage appears whereas in others the normal voltage changes. Such changes affect the flow of the circulatory system in that area as a result of electrostriction.

I feel that I must say a few words about electrostriction. It is an aspect of piezoelectricity[6]. If a mechanical pressure is applied on two faces of certain crystals, the electrical charges on the other faces will be found to increase. Vice versa, if an electrical charge is applied to the latter faces, a stress or striction will be exerted upon the former faces. Now, may I remind you that biological cells and fluids, under certain conditions, have a semi-crystalline or even a completely crystalline structure. In addition, the red blood corpuscles have a pyroelectric effect—that is, if one applies an electrical charge to some points, an increased temperature will occur at other points. What is the effect of "electrostriction" on fluids?

The diagram (Figure 4) shows this effect. If a voltage is applied to the plate of the condenser a, then the water b surrounding the condenser will exert a striction effect upon the air bubble c in the middle of the condenser. In turn, the air within the bubble communicates with the pressure gauge d and the water in the capillary tube e. As a result, the gauge will measure the pressure effect and the water in e will flow out of the orifice f.

From this it is obvious that a voltage applied to a certain place on an organism will affect the flow of fluids in the surrounding tissues, producing a stress in the local environment. The pattern of such a stress will differ from place to place in accordance with the structure of the tissue affected by the voltage.

Thus, for instance, the same voltage will produce a different stress pattern in the liver than in the adrenal gland and the supply of nutriments will be correspondingly affected. In disease, therefore, the abnormal electrical state of the affected organs will interfere with the circulation through them. If the electrical state is restored to normality by suitable inter-positions of the therapist's hand, the normal electrical state and the normal circulation through those organs will be restored.

Such an electrical approach to the human body should enable us to introduce mathematics into the problems of clinical medicine.

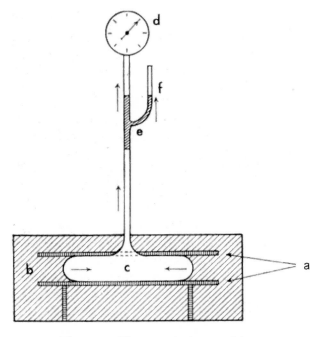

Figure 4: Electrostriction model

Practical methods of curing by hands

The consideration of such theoretical assumptions prompted the writer to attempt practical treatment. In accordance with the above described theories, the whole system of treatment was named, Psycho-Physical Field Therapy. The psychological aspects have been eliminated here for lack of space. I shall refer only occasionally to them, though I must mention that as a result of the researches of Hans Selye of the University of Montreal, Canada[7], it is quite obvious that emotions are the cause of many ailments, and also have a significant influence on the electrical side of dysfunctions; likewise the treatment of such dysfunctions.

With relatively short training, anybody can become sensitive to the so called disturbances around the body, which are manifestations of the electrostatic field, by simply moving the hand up and down *slowly*, starting from the vicinity of the body and gradually moving away to a distance of about six feet away; or vice versa. Some people pick this up at once, whilst others require preliminary training. It took the writer several months before he became conscious of these disturbances: a prickling, coolness, heat or heaviness. Different people apparently react differently to disturbances. The sensation is actually so faint that it requires great concentration. It is easiest if a definite disturbed region of the body is chosen, such as the heart or liver, before proceeding to discern these disturbances. The cause of these disturbances is the superimposition of separate waves of electrical forces producing an interference pattern. They may also manifest as thermal waves in the infra-red spectrum, that can be photographed by infra-red cameras[8].

Now, we can ask, why are such sensations actually detectable with the hand? The explanation is that the hand has its own normal electrical field which is especially strong around the tips of the fingers, because electricity always tends to flow from more pointed parts. By approaching the hand towards the body of a patient, we introduce our own field into that of the patient, producing an interference of the two. This interference is felt at the tips of the fingers as a sensation that is registered in the brain. My more recent researches have shown that a sort of feed-back mechanism is probably present, controlling the sensitivity of the fingers.

In order to distinguish the normal field from the disturbed one, our attention must be focused on this very disturbance, so that we may increase the awareness of the sensation at our fingertips. Only in this way will we be able to discern the quality of the disturbance. This skill of course improves with training, just as the ability to discern pathological sounds of the human body improves with practise at auscultation.

It has been found in experiments that the extent of the disturbed field varies with the intensity of the disturbances in the body. A severe disturbance can be felt further away than a minor one. This is in good accordance with theoretical considerations, for the displacement of charges increases with the intensity of the disturbance. A malfunctioning organ creates a greater disturbance than a normal one because of the increase of the charge involved. As a result of this increased charge associated with malfunction, increased sensation is apparent in the hand of the investigator.

G. T. Fechner[9] found that the relationship between the stimulus and the sensation could be described by the logarithmic law:

$$I = c^* \text{Log } s$$

where I stands for the sensation, s for the stimulus estimated in numbers, and c for a constant that varies between different persons, but remains the same for each individual.

Once the distinct sensation is well-established in the hand of the investigator, we can proceed to actual treatment. In the preceding theory, the field surrounding the body is a function of the metabolic state of the cells. The reverse is also true, that the cells are influenced by the field. It would then follow that any alteration of this field should cause a corresponding response in the body and in the malfunctioning organ. Experiments show that this is what actually happens. The reaction in the patient is sometimes so strong that he distinctly feels that something is happening in the region of the disturbance. Actually if that does not happen in the patient, it is an indication that the cure will be difficult.

The problem arises, how can we alter the field by our hands? For the purpose of clarity, let us again simplify this complicated problem. We have assumed that a malfunctioning organ has a surplus of positive charges. Hence a surplus of negative charges will accumulate in the air surrounding the organ, through the attraction of opposite charges. Then, if the hand, which acts as a capacitor, is introduced into the surrounding air (field) it will adsorb the excess negative charges. By repeating this action, withdrawing the hand each time and rubbing against a cloth or similar material, the surplus charge will be eliminated and the normal function of the organ restored. It has been found that the same thing can be done by introducing a moist sponge into the field, which will also adsorb the excess charges. However, the sponge must be rinsed thoroughly after each introduction into the field, whilst the excess charge on the hand can be merely rubbed off. What is most peculiar is that it appears that the hand has a much greater electrical adsorbing capacity than any kind of sponge. It is well known that a sponge has a very large total surface area, including the complicated network of cavities within it. When moist, all of the surfaces are covered by a thin film of water, which carries an electrical charge and therefore adsorbs opposite charges by simple attraction. The whole moist sponge can therefore adsorb a large quantity of charge. This adsorbed charge is dispersed by thorough rinsing in water. In contrast, the hand has only a small surface area. Obviously other factors must also operate, but what is their nature?

It has been found in practise, that one must start with the most distant layer of disturbances at the perimeter of the field and clear it before proceeding more proximally. A cleared field is indicated when there is a complete lack of any sensation in the hand. If a sponge is used, the process is tedious because the hand must be interposed frequently in order to determine whether the field is clear or not. If one attempts to clear a field without starting at the periphery, nothing will be achieved. The reason for this is not yet known.

Practise has shown that after a field has been completely cleared right down to the patient's skin, the patient feels much better, though after a period of time (hours or days) the disturbances may return. However they are much weaker than before. The field must be cleared again, though much less work has to be done the second time. Once the field is cleared, the patient is cured. Sometimes the treatment takes only a few minutes, but stubborn cases may take several hours. Nonetheless, the patient sometimes feels that he has been cured instantaneously and regards his recovery as a miracle, but as is evident from the above discussion, it is not. In chronic cases the disturbances return, though their intensity is much less than that of acute illness. They must be removed again and recurrences often occur several times.

A well trained and sensitive therapist soon finds that the procedure of feeling sensations by placing his hand in the field, repeatedly removing it, then discarding the surplus charges, becomes automatic. He automatically removes his hands as soon as he feels that the adsorbing power is saturated, and rubs them off on a cloth or washes them off in water. If the therapist does not so remove the charges acquired from the patient, he himself becomes affected. At the conclusion of the treatment, he must wash his hands thoroughly in cold water, so that no residual charge remains. If he does not take these precautions, he will at first get a sensation of heaviness in his hand, possibly pain. If he takes no notice, the sensation will spread up his arm and the rest of his body will become affected giving him headaches and a feeling of uneasiness. If the therapist suffers from the same disease as the patient, he will experience similar pains. For instance, if they both have heart disease, the therapist will experience chest pains. Therapists are usually able to cure themselves of such pains by the same techniques they use on the patients.

For some unknown reason the field surrounding the diseased organ is not always composed of layers of intensity increasing from the periphery to the skin surface (as described above). The *whole* field may be uniformly dense. Such cases are difficult to cure and require long and tedious treatment. During the treatment, the field ceases to be uniformly dense and becomes layered in intensity, like that of less difficult cases. Eventually a complete cure is achieved. According to mathematical analyses of the harmonics involved in the field, if too many harmonics are present, the field may become a dense cloud of charges, resulting in the uniform denseness detected by the hand.

After more than twenty years of methodical investigations, it has been found that patients can be treated at a distance with some success. The author was formerly very sceptical of such claims by so-called healers until he actually observed it in practise. It was proved to him by the following procedure. A patient was chosen who had a disease which could not be cured by normal medical treatment. In order to eliminate suggestion, neither did the patient know that he was going to be treated, nor did anyone else. Thus, no knowledge of the treatment could have been passed to the patient. The patient was treated for a few days at a distance. Then it was stopped. It was repeated at varying periods of time. The patient felt worse or better according to whether he was being treated or not. Since the possibilities of suggestion and chance had been virtually excluded, his improvement was due to the treatment itself. Similar experiments were made with many other patients with the same results. What is the explanation of this phenomenon?

We come here to the psychological factor. It has been known for a long time that one of the main factors in such treatment is the visualization of the therapist. He must either see the patient or must have a distinct picture of him in him in his mind. A successful result can only be achieved if the therapist can accurately imagine the field of the distant patient. Then and only then can a patient be cured at a distance. The therapist can aid the patient in his recovery if he imagines him recovering from his illness. The more intense the image, the quicker the recovery.

This very fact brings added difficulties to explaining the phenomenon in terms of the above hypothesis of static electrical fields. One can perhaps postulate that an interference pattern occurs in the patient's field, who may be 100 miles or more from the therapist. Or, is such treatment a manifestation of telepathy?

Here we must mention experiments performed by one of the professors of the Lviv Lemberg Technical University in Poland. Those experiments were conducted with Paramecium, a Protozoan. He placed them on a microscope slide and observed them for several months. When the slide dried, they became encapsulated; but the capsule was discarded as soon as water was poured on it. Once, this professor happened to leave the Paramecia dry for several weeks and observed them at the end of that time. They were still encapsulated. He decided to pour some water on the slide. However, he looked at them again just before he poured the water onto them, and to his astonishment saw that they had already discarded their capsules. How on Earth could they have known that he was going to pour on the water? Then he decided not to give them any water. After a short space of time he looked again and found the Paramecia had again encapsulated. This was more than astonishing. Had they actually responded to his thought? The experiment was repeated many times and every time the response was positive. He then phoned a colleague at Warsaw University, and asked him to phone any time he chose, ordering him to pour water onto the Paramecia. The Warsaw colleague thought that this suggestion was strange, but after a short argument agreed. A few days later he rang the Lviv professor and told him to pour the water onto the Paramecia. Immediately the latter ran to them to see if they had acted upon the Warsaw colleague's thoughts. They had! (They took longer to encapsulate than he took to run to them).

This latter experiment is repeatable, provided that the experimenter works with the animals for a certain time. This experiment shows that at least small organisms respond to human thought. Hence, why shouldn't the constituent cells of an animal, or at least the tissues and organs, respond also? This suggestion correlates well with the finding recorded above, namely that when treating patients at a distance, the best results are achieved when the whole patient is well-visualised in the mind of the therapist.

A full psychological explanation would entail a long and separate paper. The fact though remains that distance therapy is possible, and in fact it is the function of the creative imagination (as distinct from fantasy). By such processes of the imagination the subject can go anywhere he likes; because, to the imagination, space and time are not limiting factors. Actually, we go on such expeditions quite often, in dreams. We see a distant place where we have never been before. When we actually go there, we find it familiar. Then we recall that we saw it in our dream. Similar phenomena happen with time. We may sometimes see events several days in advance, which manifest several days later. The psychology of the collective subconscious and archetypes offers an answer to this problem.

Further researches have proved that such possibilities of treatment at distance are not a *gift* given to only certain persons. On the contrary almost everyone can, when properly trained, be successful. It is estimated that eight persons out of ten can produce therapeutic results after proper training. There is a whole science behind this, and it can hardly be called *faith healing*. Hard work and proper knowledge are what lead to results. Can such facts be explained in terms of static electrical fields? If not, then the whole of the hypothesis outlined above is false. From Dr. Hans Selye's work, we know that emotions have a prominent place in the cause of disease. Thus they must have a dominant influence on the redistribution of electrical charges in the body. A simple encephalogram shows this clearly, changing with the mood of the patient. Hence, changes in the psychology of a subject cause changes in the electrical field. There is in fact a strict correlation between the psychological factors and the pattern of the electrical field.

Suppose now that a subject's thoughts and imagination are centred upon a distant person. In doing so, he transfers all his emotional influence to the distant person; because his imagination is intimately related to his personality. So, although the body of the therapist remains at its location, he is, in his imagination, at the distant place in front of the patient. He senses the psychological tensions of the patient and suitably restores them to normal. Once the emotional disturbances are restored to normal, a normal redistribution of electrical charges can occur in the body of the patient and normal health results.

At first sight, such a conception seems to be very far-fetched. However, after careful consideration it becomes conceivable, and eventually feasible. By such a process, small changes in the electrical field of the patient (measurable only in micro-volts or even millivolts), may not only be sensed, but also influenced. The experiments with Paramecium support this idea. Therefore, in order to explain telepathy, there is no need to resort to unknown powers; but simply to see it as a function of the imagination acting in conjunction with sensation. Besides, anyone, properly trained, may achieve definite results.

What the author claims in this article has been proved by reliable scientific researches. Working hypotheses were initially formulated and substantiated by controlled and repeatable experiments. The author believes that if a team of scientists, such as physicists, biophysicists, psychologists and open-minded medical doctors, were to continue this research, they would definitely arrive at a greater understanding of this topic.

14

THE MUSIC OF CRYSTALS, PLANTS AND HUMAN BEINGS[1]

Introduction

Just as the driver of a car recognises through noises produced by the engine whether it is running correctly or not, so also any medical doctor knows very well how great a part sound plays in his medical diagnosis. Whether he percusses with his finger the body of his patient, or uses the stethoscope, it is always sound in its various forms which will give him the required information.

Robert Hooke, an English physicist, wrote in the late 17th century that "it may be possible to discover the motions of the internal parts of bodies, whether *animal, vegetable, or mineral* (italics mine), by the sound they make; that one may discover the works performed in the several offices and shops of a man's body, and thereby discover what instrument or engine is out of order, what works are going on at several times, and lie still at others, and the like; that in plants and vegetables one might discover by the noise of the pumps for raising the juice, the valves for stopping it, and the rushing of it out of one passage into another, and the like?"[2] This text can hardly be emphasised enough. Unfortunately its implications have been ignored up to the present time.

It is quite evident that the flow of the blood, the beating of the heart, or the functioning of any organ must produce a sound because friction is constantly present. This sound, as Hooke noted, can be compared to the hum of a factory, and by its quality one will be able to find out what is actually going on inside the factory. There is no need to say more about this fundamental truth.

Is the stethoscope which medical doctors constantly use, or the percussing by the finger of the chest or abdomen, a sensitive enough instrument for modern requirements? It is not intended here to argue about the simplicity of these instruments which can be carried in any doctor's pocket. Neither shall we deny that the human ear is extremely sensitive to a narrow wave-band of sound in the range of about 2,500 Hz. But for higher or lower frequencies, the human ear is either very inefficient, or even completely deaf. It is very possible that just these particular sounds are the most important. The pulse of the heart is extremely low, and it is still the most fundamental. Actually all life pulses, as experience teaches us, are very slow. These pulses are entirely below the threshold of hearing. Others, which are above the audible range, on the contrary, produce often deadly effects, or they are at least very dangerous. We mean here ultrasonic sounds. From this cursory inspection of the problem it is evident how very important it is to get exact information about these particular sounds in the organism. The present technical developments of our age should easily provide a satisfactory means not only to amplify the quality of these sounds, but also to show us their actual picture on a cathode ray tube. In other words to show the quality of the sound in a pictorial way.

Theoretically speaking this could be displayed in a two-fold manner. One could show the actual wave-form on the screen, with its very complicated peaks and sharp turnings. Or else one could show the interference pattern resulting from thousands of waves superimposed on one another. Let us explain this. It is enough to set two sources of waves on a surface of a still water, to see such a wave interference pattern. (Figure 5)

There are crests and troughs, rows in between, and they are perfectly symmetrical. Now imagine this in three dimensions. Let us pass a strong beam of light through this pattern so that all the condensed nodes will light up as small stars. You will then get a network looking actually exactly as an X-Ray pattern of a crystalline lattice produced by the Laue method. (Figure 6)

If we imagine further that all these flickering star-points—according to their amplitude and frequency interferences, their beats, pulses or periodic scintillations—will assume different colours and

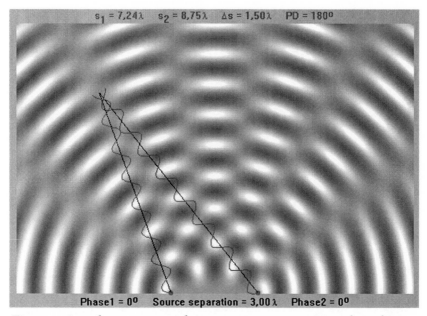

Figure 5: Interference pattern from two wave sources. Note the radiating lines where two wave patterns cancel each other out and the double crests between them.

shades, then you will have a picture of a sound interference pattern, but instead of seeing lights and their colours, you will hear a beautiful harmonic music. Such music, apart from its melody and orchestration, will have in addition a morphological shape. It will have a structural and architectural appearance. Modern techniques should provide us with the means to project such patterns on a cathode ray tube. An investigation of these patterns or wave-forms should be a perfect means of providing information of what is going on in the organism and organs of the human body. It should enable doctors to give an exact diagnosis. As a skilled physiologist looking at a microscope slide of a tissue immediately recognises what tissue he is dealing with, so exactly the same should be possible from the wave interference pattern or wave-form, as seen on a cathode ray tube. Any distortion in such pattern will inform the modern doctor that there is something wrong.

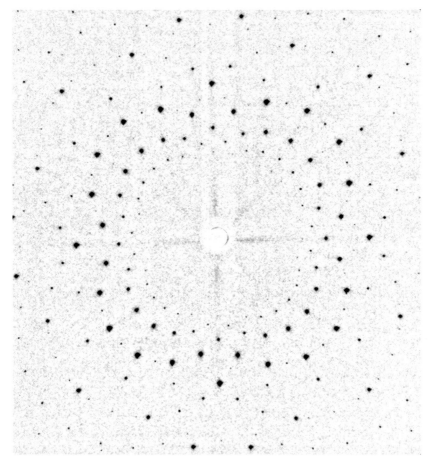

Figure 6: X-ray diffraction Pattern of a crystal using the Laue method

The Music of Crystals

Before we enter on a discussion of crystals themselves, let us first define what is meant by music. One single note, e.g., middle *c*, is not itself music. This is only periodical vibration in time, called a tone. When we hear a collection of tones, which follow one another in time, we may call it a tune or melody, and when tones appear together then it can be a chord.

If these collections of tones are not properly and proportionately related, then they produce a noise, but when the proportionality is preserved, then our ear appreciates it, and it appeals to us as music. We can see immediately that the meaning of the word music is essentially related to a certain proportionality between a collection of notes. This proportionality could be described also as a correct relationship or proper relativity between two or more motions; periodic motions. The word *proper* implies an evaluation of these proportions, which evaluation is a purely mental process. Nevertheless, instead of using the expression "proper relationship" or "relativity," it is preferred to stick to the word proportionality, which renders the meaning better.

These proportions or proportionalities can be represented by numbers. Thus the relationship of the middle c (on the piano keyboard) which has 256 c/sec. to itself, can be written as 256/256. If we accept this as the point of reference, then it can be written as 1/1. The ratio of its first harmonic, the octave to C, numerically is written 512/256, and can be represented as 2/1; the next harmonic, the g, will be given by 3/1, and so forth. We have thus a divergent series, 1/1, 2/1., 3/1, 4/1 ...n/1. Such representation can be used for any number, so long as their ratios are harmonically related. Thus 512,000 c/sec. to 256,000 c/sec. can also be given by the ratio 2/1, etc. We see then that the relationship between colossal or minute numbers can be reduced to a very simple numerical form. As has been said, this ratio is evaluated by a purely mental process, and the mind does not bother as to whether its perception is of billions or only a few cycles per second, whether the ratio is astronomical or atomic in size ; what is essential is the harmonic ratio and its value[3].

In music this sequence of tones harmonically related is named by letters, as *c, d, e, f* and so forth. We must remember that these tones bear a numerical relationship of periodic motions in time to the fundamental tone from which we start. In any C major scale it will be the *c.* Hence, the name of a tone, for instance *g*, does not mean the quantity of periodic motions in a unit of time, as there are several *g*'s in the keyboard, and each of them has a different frequency. The name *g* represents a relationship to another tone, and this relationship is evaluated mentally. It is not only a quantity nor a pure physical fact; it represents also a mental process. This statement is most important for the understanding of the Psycho-Physical Law of Fechner-Weber. In what we call *music* the perception of the physical fact is closely related to a mental process of evaluation[4].

If we take the numerical proportionalities only, then these proportions are called in music, *intervals*, as for instance an, octave; a fifth, fourth, a third, etc. The mental process of evaluation relates them immediately to the fundamental tone, the very moment a sequence of such intervals, harmonically related, is played. It is these proportionalities and their possible sequences which are evaluated and perceived by the ear and involve the mental process. When such a sequence fits with our own standard of proportions, we label it as correct, nice or beautiful, but when such a collection of tones does not harmonise with our own standard, inborn in our minds, then we call it a noise or a discord. Why we have an inborn standard, and the nature of this mechanism of pleasing and displeasing chords, is a different problem and will not be dealt with here.

This fundamental fact of perception of proportions was thoroughly analysed a long time ago by the two scientists Fechner and Weber, and it led them finally to the formulation of the well-known Fechner-Weber Psycho-Physical Law[4]. This law can be applied not only to hearing, but also to vision, and mutatis mutandis to other senses, as in all of them the mental process of evaluation of proportions is involved. When we realise that proportions and contrasts are the essential features of every art, then it becomes evident that the Psycho-Physical law of Fechner-Weber introduces us to the realm of art and beauty. The physical facts and their mental evaluation are here brought into unity, and open to us a new world for scientific psychophysical investigation. It happens that we prefer to call it psychosomatic research.

About a hundred years ago a Berlin crystallographer called Weiss[5] showed that the angles in crystals, the proportions between their sides and planes could be represented by musical relationships. This idea was taken up by a German scientist, Victor Goldschmidt. In his book, *Über Harmonie und Komplikation* (On Harmony and

Complication)[6], he showed by all sorts of matrices and exact measurements, that the harmonic music principle plays an essential part in the world of crystals and their growth. Different crystals follow different musical scales and tones, such as E sharp major, E flat minor, etc. They have separate collections of tones, and along their co-ordinate axes they show different motifs for polyphony and contra points. The axes of the crystals are the points of reference in these measurements of proportions. Hans Kayser aptly calls them the "crystal tuning forks."[7]

The essential reason for such musical representation of crystals lies in the nature of molecules and atoms; in the basic construction of matter. *Atoms are known to be harmonic oscillators*, where the oscillators themselves are the nuclei, and the electrons and their orbits are, may we call them, the reverberation and echoes of the periodic harmonic motions of the nucleus. Actually the electrons represent the peaks or condensed nodes in the wave interference pattern, and the orbits (and we must not forget this) are the nodal points of the standing waves surrounding any atom. It is music on the atomic scale, and the musical proportionalities are perfectly preserved there. The quanta and their integral numbers with their boundary conditions and energy states leave no doubt about it. The electrons and their shells are the function of the nuclear oscillations and vice versa. They are all a sort of double chorus playing alternately their musical proportions. From the very foundations of the atoms, up to stars and galaxies the harmonic law of proportions is the fundamental one. Kepler introduced it into astronomy in his work *Harmonices Mundi*, whilst nuclear physics discusses it in terms of atoms.

This fundamental law of harmony is perceived by human beings as proportions and their musical relationship. Whether the distances are astronomical in size, or minute as atoms and sub-atomic particles, the proportions are always the same, and can be represented by simple figures, as already stated 1/2, 5/4...called in music, *intervals*. They can also be labelled with musical names, *e, g, f, d*... There is no need to be a great expert in physics and philosophy in order to see that these proportionalities can be applied not only to the material world, but also to the immaterial one, as this perception of proportion is essentially a mental process. It has been shown before and we repeat it here again—the Psycho-Physical Law is the basis. It links together soul and body, mind and matter, God and Creation. It is the law of Beauty and therefore is related to Goodness and Truth. *Pulchrum, Bonum, Verum.* The Supreme Being as Beauty, Goodness and Truth must be reflected throughout Creation.

In psychosomatics this Psycho-Physical Law must be the starting point of all real and orthodox scientific research.

Let us return to our crystals. It is well known that they contain a splendid network, in physics usually called a lattice, of atoms and molecules which co-ordinate themselves according to their specific axes, and produce the resulting shape, the morphological appearance of the crystal[8].

A question arises now whether such crystals are surrounded with any actual real musical field? Does a mechanical vibration of a sonic nature surround it? We must consider this more closely.

It is known that the molecules of a crystal have only certain freedoms of vibration. They can move only in certain directions, or, say, along certain axes. Putting it a different way, their thermal agitation is polarised more in one direction than in others. Such general motion of particles over a surface of a crystal will produce also a similar one in the molecules of the surrounding gas, e.g., the air. An artificially forced vibration induced in such a crystal can produce a very strong beam in the air. Some ultrasonic beams of such vibration can kill a rat at a distance of 100 yards. Normally there is no such forced vibration in crystals in their natural state. Their periodic motion is a free vibration of an extremely faint nature. This vibration being also a mechanical one will of course have a sonic character, although it may not be audible, simply because it may be too faint in the audible range. To a certain extent the vibration of a crystal can be amplified by simply knocking it. This can be done with any object, and it will produce a noise according to its shape, size, chemical nature, state of tension and so forth. We must remember though that in such a case we hear the resultant of two noises, that from knocking the object and that from the object knocked. While every object has different modes of vibration, we usually hear only one component, the object's natural vibration. A better example of amplification of the natural vibration of, e.g., glass, is when a singer hits the glass' natural note and shatters it to fragments. This due to the principle of resonance. If the singer could produce by his voice all the vibrations of the components of the glass, a complete disintegration would follow. The released energy would be colossal.

Are there any electrical components of such vibration? J. C. Bose showed a long time ago that a mechanical impulse involves electrical currents. We know from piezoelectricity of crystals, that any mechanical change of pressure on the Y axis is accompanied by a proportional change of electrical voltage along the X axis. Latest reports seem to attribute piezoelectric phenomena —though very weak ones—to all objects. This is in exact agreement with what J. C. Bose showed in his numerous experiments[9].

The exact opposite, namely, that alternating currents produce mechanical phenomena, was shown by a French scientist named Ludin. He proved that when a metal wire is heated by an alternating current a sound may be heard, having a frequency double that of the alternating periodicity of the applied current[10]. This is illustrated in the following curve (Figure 7), where the sine wave represents the electrical frequency (transverse component) and the vertical lines denote the mechanical, longitudinal component. We see that the frequency of one is double the other. As a matter of fact, here is the actual physical reason why harmonics appear in any wave motion[11].

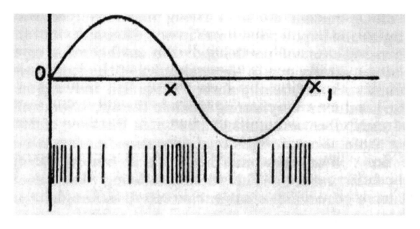

Figure 7: Diagrammatic representation of a longitudinal sound wave. The vertical bars indicate maximum and minimum air compression. The sine wave represents the electrical component.

We know that any frequency creates its harmonics, but as far as my knowledge goes, the exact physical mechanism of it has never been shown. It is due to the close relationship and connecting link between the transverse and longitudinal component of *any wave motion*. From the experiment quoted above we see that electromagnetic and mechanical phenomena are strictly interrelated. Mathematically I have shown this generally in "The Gravitational Wave"[18]. Its application in the case of light, an electromagnetic wave, was demonstrated in the experiments of Prof. Ehrenhaft[12].

Returning to crystals, based on the fine structures of the fields of their atoms and molecules, their overall field is electromagnetic as well as mechanical. It is then quite evident that if we change periodically the mutual position of molecules and atoms, a similar periodic change will occur between their electromagnetic fields, so emitting an electromagnetic wave. A mechanical, periodic molecular vibration must give rise to a periodic, electromagnetic wave. As a matter of fact infra-red radiation emitted by all matter is partly of such a nature. Does not heat arise from the mechanical motion of thermal agitation? Now, if such thermal agitation is restricted in a certain direction due to its mechanical motion, it will produce a sonic wave. This is just what is to be expected in crystals, where the freedom of vibration of molecules is restricted to certain directions.

It is also well known that in a great many crystals we find the three axes X, Y and Z: the electrical, the mechanical and the optical. This is due to the fact that all the molecules of crystals are axially arranged together with their harmonic proportionalities. Hence the field surrounding the crystal will not be an isotropic one, but definitely anisotropic. Along the Y axis we shall expect mainly the mechanical phenomena to appear, along the X axis the electrostatic, and along the Z axis perpendicular to the other two, light—an electromagnetic phenomenon, will operate. We may find here reason for Reichenbach's claims that light emitted from the top and bottom of crystals was visible to sensitive persons[13]. He succeeded even in photographing this light. But as in those days there was no theoretical explanation of such a possibility, the whole thing was entirely dropped. Now, in the light of modern knowledge, this phenomenon seems to have a reasonable foundation.

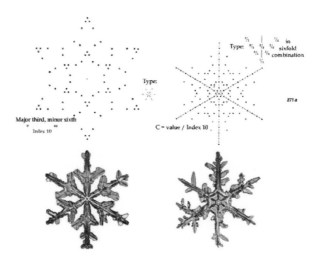

Figure 8: Photographs of Snow Crystals and the matrix of harmonic intervals. From *Grundriss eines Systems der Harmonikalen Werdformen* by Hans Hayser.

To end this short discussion about crystals and their proportionalities, it would perhaps be worthwhile to show some pictures of snow crystals taken from the microphotos in H. Kayser's book, *Grundriss eines Systems der Harmonikalen Werdformen* (Occidentverlag, Zurich, 1946), and compare them with matrices of musical proportionalities made for the possible interference between two or more tones and their harmonies. (Figure 8). From this comparison we may easily form a more exact picture of how musical harmonic proportions can be present in the morphological appearance of crystals.

The music of plants

We pass now to the next subject, plants. From everyday experience we know that plants grow according to proportions which are proper and particular to each of their species. These proportions can be easily measured and represented by numbers. Kayser in his most interesting book *Harmonia Plantarum*[14] showed how these proportions can be perfectly represented by musical intervals and tones, as well as how they follow the harmonic law in their growth.

According to this law, if we strike middle-*c* on the piano keyboard and release the damper from the strings, its first sub-harmonic below will be *c*, one octave lower, the second sub-harmonic *f*, then *c* again. If we go further, we hear a minor sequence of notes. Our mental evaluation reveals that this is a minor scale. Numerically this sequence is represented by 1/1, 1/2, 1/3, ¼...1/n. If instead of going down from the middle *c* we go up, the harmonic sequence is represented numerically as 1/1, 2/1, 3/1 4/1...n/1 and our ear perceives them as a major scale. One is the mirror of the other. Generally speaking, on striking any tone on the keyboard, the harmonic sequences will always follow the same sequences of major or minor scales. The dividing point is the tone which has been struck, from which the harmonics are counted toward both ends. For more details we refer the reader, to the excellent works of Kayser from which the above was learned. It is necessary to mention that every tone assumes a certain angle relative to the fundamental tone.

If we would represent the numerical values of the above sequences by respective sections in length and their angles, then, taking all the above factors into account, the resultant picture represents schematically the exact shape of a plant. Excellent drawings are given by Kayser in his *Harmonia Plantarum* on pages 27, 82, 41. The dividing point is the one at the surface of the earth, the point of germination. The proportions above the ground follow the major scale, and below, the minor one. Of course they can be represented by musical notes, as actually Kayser did, drawing them beneath the schematic design mentioned. (Figure 9 and Kayser's footnotes). Such representations of sectors gives us a good picture of the growth of the stem and the roots. If we now imagine this in three dimensions we have the perfect shape of a plant.

One of the most important observations is that the proportions which the growth of plants follow, do not correspond to the numerical value of frequencies. On the contrary they follow a logarithmic law, the same law which underlies the ear's evaluation. This evaluation, as it was said, is purely a mental process, and is the basis of Fechner-Weber's Psycho-Physical Law. Strangely enough the growth of the plant is governed by the same law. It follows, as Kayser demonstrated, not a material impulse, (he calls it *of pure quantity*), but the mental impulse of value[15]. In other words it grows according to the same law which governs the world of art and not that of pure quantities.

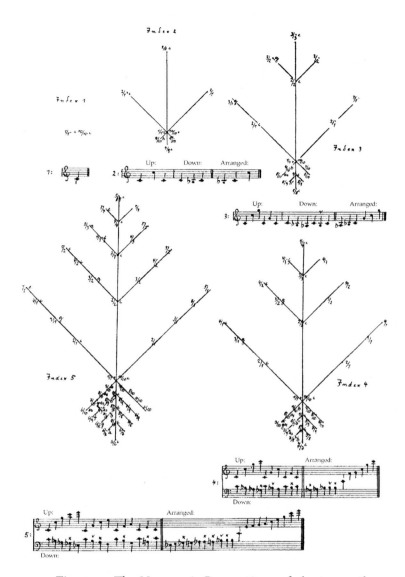

Figure 9: The Harmonic Proportions of plant growth
from Hans Kayser's "Harmonia Plantarum"*

---

* The plant is based on paleobotanical plant Sigillaria, a proto-tree that flourished in
the Carboniferous era. Kayser argues that this proto-tree is the geometrical model
for subsequent trees.

A further interesting detail is that one can find the differences of the phases between particular tones and frequencies in the way the offshoots from the stem grow in any particular plant, from which the true shape of the plant results. A great deal could be written about these phase differences, but this would lead us too far. We have to refer the reader again to the works of Kayser[16].

It is easily seen that a seed is not a random accumulation of matter, but a well organised one. Hence only certain freedoms of vibration are permissible and, in the whole seed, the directions are axially polarised, just as they are in any crystal. This freedom of vibration along some specific axis will depend on the chemical combinations existing in the seed and their chemical bond. The resultant pattern of these vibrations and molecular arrangement, if amplified, will influence the growth of the plant.

Now, let us suppose that, for instance in a plant seed of a particular species we have a combination of three fundamental proportionalities, or simply tones, thanks to their chemical constitution. They may be the *c, g,* and *e,* which form a major fifth, the *c-g,* a major third

---

Kayser's Notes on the diagram:

Index 1 is the as yet undeveloped "seed" 1/1 *c*; two elements are dormant in it: size and limitation, symbolized by index 10/10, and its inner value, symbolized by the generator-tone c=1/1.

Index 2 shows the initial "germination" and with it the beginning formation of the root and stem. Whereas the "above-ground" formation is still entirely within the kernel value (only c-values, seed leaves), the below-ground part shows a new value (*b*) and thus the differentiation of the beginning root growth.

Index 3 progresses upwards towards further bifurcation in large fifth interval steps (g), while at the bottom the root region gives birth to two new values, *b*" and a♭

Index 4 contains the second fifth f in the upper part, and in the lower part the ratios of 7, g.♭, a♭, and b♭

Index 5, by contrast, produces new value both above and below, as the notation shows.

In examining the tone-value excerpts, especially comparing the arranged index tones, one will notice that at first (index 2) the "above-ground" part grows in octaves, while the "underground" part only moves in whole-tones. In the further progression of the following indexes, this tendency toward large intervals above and small intervals below appears to increase. But if one examines this development more closely, one will note that for index 5, there is also a tendency toward narrower intervals above, and toward larger intervals below. These two tendencies also become visible through the graphic images of the diagrams because their logarithmic arrangements are dictated by the tones and not by the numbers!

and a minor one, *c-e* and *e-g*. These tones will have different frequencies and different harmonics according to their pitch. They may also have different amplitudes or intensities. A combination of these tones, thanks to their interference, will produce a definite pattern in three dimensions. It would be enough to amplify these mechanical vibrations which lie hidden in the seed—where this vibration is extremely minute and faint—in order to produce the germination of the seed. This amplification can be compared to the example given above, of a singer singing in resonance with a glass. The glass breaks into pieces when the amplitudes of the molecules become too large, for it cannot grow. On the contrary, the plant being a living thing begins to grow, but it will grow according to the particular interference pattern of its component tones, the amplitudes which have been increased. The cause of the amplification, which increases the momentum of the molecules (which is dependent on their freedom of vibration), is light. The molecules will react differently to its different wavelengths. We know that the infra-red band of the light spectrum increases the momentum of molecules by thermal agitation. We see why heat is indispensable for the plant's growth. Other frequencies of the light spectrum will produce analogous effects in their wavelength range.

Ehrenhaft's photophoresis, and his latest experiments with graphite dust, leave no doubt about this effect of light (Figure 10)[17]. This aspect of the problem explains in one stroke a great many facts. Briefly, the increase of the momentum is due to the pressure of light along the so-called Poynting's Vector and the longitudinal component of light, about which more details have been given in the writer's paper, "The Gravitational Wave"[18].

From the combinations of the possible freedoms of the vibration (due to the chemical bond, etc.) of the seeds, different patterns will result, and the growing plants will assume different shapes, and result in different morphological forms. We see that the shape of the plant, the peculiar shape of the species, results from the interference pattern of the combinations of mechanical waves, which we usually call "sounds." From different collections of tones, intervals and their amplitudes, specific shapes will emerge. Such shapes are literally music encapsulated in form and matter.*

---

* Later Andrew modified this hypothesis by introducing Stromberg's Primary Field as the field that determines the morphological development of all growing (and non-living) things. However the biological function of the morphogenetic field remains the same.

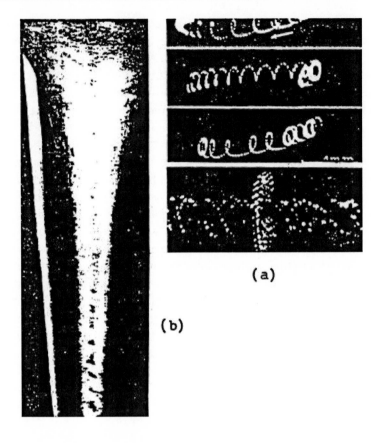

(a)

(b)

Figure 10: Motion of graphite particles irradiated by light.
From Ehrenhaft's experiment at the University of Vienna.

Of course the environment of the growing plant will have something to say here as well. In different positions and environments, slight changes in the details of the shape will appear. But the fundamentals will not change. Actually the very root and basis of genetics are found here.

Considering all these factors, and accepting them as a working hypothesis for a possible solution to these most interesting problems, it was concluded that the sap of the plant must essentially contain the same vibratory combinations as the plant. By crystallising the sap one would expect that the shape of the crystal will correspond in some way to the morphological appearance of the plant from which the sap was taken. Therefore specimens were taken and examined under the microscope. In several cases of very typical plant shapes, the results were definitely positive. The best examples were obtained with the sap taken from the leaf of Yarrow, or otherwise called Milfoil (Achillea Millefolium), Nasturtium or Indian Cress (Tropaeolum Maius) and Dandelion (Tarawacum Officinale). The sap was simply dropped on the microscopic slide and permitted to dry and crystallise. This proves that the principle is not without foundation, at least in some eases. We leave the more exact determination to specialists. One curious phenomenon was observed. In order to obtain these crystalline patterns, the sap had to be put on the slide shortly after the plant has been picked. Also better results were obtained when the plants were picked after rain than during a dry spell.

From these results and the logical trend of thought, we may presume that the future shape of any plant is concealed in the vibratory motions of the seed. It is also believed that the general lines given above can be accepted at least as a working hypothesis.

The Music of the Human Organism

Before approaching the subject the reader is asked to remember that the problem is purposely simplified in order not to blur the general picture with details.

We may pass now to the human body. It has been shown in the introductory part that the human organism must be surrounded with a sound which is the function of the molecular agitation going on in the organs. We can easily see that each organ will have its own sonic field—its own noise—which, if properly detected, should provide us with information of the processes going on in them. We should also keep in mind that the human body, as well as its particular organs, is not a heap of matter accumulated at random, but a well-organised entity and hence bears a sort of analogy to crystals. In scientific literature this analogy has long been suggested.

The first question which presents itself to an investigator is, can it actually be demonstrated that our reasoning as to the presumed sonic field of the human body is valid? Can any experiment be provided as proof?

First of all let us state clearly that these sounds must be extremely faint, otherwise our ear would detect them. Therefore a very sensitive detector must be used. In the history of physical science all sorts of devices have been invented for detecting such sounds. One of them is a sensitive flame, and another a sensitive jet. These sensitive jets have been investigated, mostly by Felix Savart and John Tyndall. They are also sometimes called sensitive veins.

Under a steady pressure you allow a water jet to flow upwards at an oblique angle. When the jet is illuminated you can see that it is surrounded by a cloud of small droplets flying in nearly all directions. It is known from Savart's and Tyndall's experiments that such jets under the influence of a sound wave in resonance with them (not all frequencies therefore will produce the effect; the selection of the frequency depends on all sorts of details) will immediately collect all these droplets into one bunch, and a definite wave pattern will appear on the jet vein itself. Please note that the wavelength of the jet does not correspond to the wavelength of the sound which produces the effect. Actually such jets are the finest sound detectors known. Remember that in using the word "sound " we mean, throughout this paper, all mechanical vibrations, in the audible range as well as ultra and infra sounds.

What does Tyndall himself write about such jets? He uses a steatite orifice to produce them, as he claims that it is far more sensitive than any other one. Here is his description:

> By means of an india-rubber tube the burner (orifice) is connected with the water pipes ... and by pointing it obliquely upwards, we obtain a fine parabolic jet. At a certain distance from the orifice, the vein resolves itself into beautiful spherules, whose motions are not rapid enough to make the vein appear continuous. At the vertex of the parabola the spray of the pearls is more than an inch across, and, further on, the drops are still more widely scattered. On sweeping a fiddle-bow across a tuning fork which executes 512 vibrations in a second, the scattered drops, as if drawn together by their mutual attractions, instantly close up, and form an apparently continuous liquid arch several feet in height and span. As long as the proper note is maintained the vein looks like a frozen band, so motionless does it appear. On stopping the fork the arch is shaken asunder, and we have the same play of liquid pearls as before. Every sweep of the bow, however, causes the drops to fall into a common line of march.

Tyndall shows further that beats between two frequencies can be actually seen on such jets[19].

It has been found by the writer that if such a jet is flowing under a very low pressure, it becomes still more sensitive. Instead of using the steatite burner or orifice, we use a simple one of metal, and the jet is produced by using an ordinary German-type primus. By pumping the air into the container and by a special screw which can regulate the opening of the tube leading to the orifice, we can thus adjust the jet itself and its pressure. The best results are obtained when the jet is not higher than about three inches.

If the human body is surrounded by a sonic field, as theoretical considerations suggest, then we should expect that a similar effect would appear on a water jet as described by Tyndall. This is what actually happens. The very moment we approach our hand, for instance, to such a jet, all the small droplets collect themselves together and the jet assumes a definite wave pattern. So long as the hand is held by the jet this wave pattern is visible. We withdraw the hand, and the spray of droplets again becomes visible.

Experiment shows, so far as one can notice with the unaided eye, that this wave pattern in the jet is not a simple sine wave, but displays rather a more complicated wave-form such as would result from hundreds of waves superimposed on one another. Such a waveform is just what would be expected, as the human sonic field is by no means a simple one. If, as Tyndall maintains, beats between two frequencies can be observed on such a jet, then in a more sensitive one a whole wave-pattern may be observable as well. Hence it is suggested that such jets should be observed by a conveniently arranged telescopic tube, set at a distance from the jet, as otherwise the sonic field of the telescope itself will affect the jet. It must be recalled that in any object the molecules are in thermal agitation, polarised by their limited freedom of vibration. Hence by summation, a sonic field should surround the object. Such a field will affect the jet. This can actually be observed by approaching any object to it. Remember, it is not the effect of temperature, as a source of heat at a distance will not affect the jet. It is also suggested that interesting results should be obtained at low temperatures with jets of liquified gases.

This fact, it is believed, gives experimental proof of our theoretical considerations. As to the possibilities of a waveform appearance on the jet, we abstain from definite statements until a telescopic observation shall actually prove it. It may happen that for every individual a different pattern will appear on the jet. Liquids other than water should be used as well. Chemical affinities and resonance principles should be observable by such methods; anyway many possibilities are open for research. We may note here that the effect on the jet of magnetic and electric fields is powerful. Lord Rayleigh noticed this with electric fields years ago[20] but no special attention was then drawn to it. As for the magnetic field, it is believed that this was not observed, and was unknown until now. The explanation is simple. In the electric as in the magnetic fields the air molecules and their thermal motions are polarised in the direction of the field, and will thus produce a resultant sonic field. When the dielectric rod is rubbed its molecules are put in vigorous motion, though inaudible to the ear. For more theoretical details we refer the reader to the notes of the writer's paper[21]. As to sensitive flames it is believed that they are not as sensitive as the jets.

The general statement can now be made that, as well as human beings, all objects radiate sound waves, and therefore their fields are sonic fields as well. Of course every individual will have his own different pattern, a different collection of tones, as the shape, the geophysical position, the state of health, etc, is different in each of us.

It must be noted that this sonic radiation will impinge upon surrounding objects, and will be partly reflected by them. Therefore, depending on our environment, a standing wave pattern should surround us, with its nodes and antinodes. As we move about in our daily life, the field of the standing wave arranges itself accordingly, and will change in some minor details, but the fundamental interference pattern of interference remain the same. The general law could be defined thus: *This radiation and its pattern is due to the distribution of the matter and its mutual correlation in any individual case.* The actual chemical nature of the matter, its temperature, shape, position and so forth, is implied by this definition. We entirely omit here the electric components of the field. Now, in light of the above, how can we explain the therapeutic results of drugs, plants, the curative effects of music, especially in some nervous diseases, etc.?

Here in our opinion we have to turn to gravity. Suppose we were to suddenly withdraw the planet Jupiter that from the planetary system? What would happen to the motions of other planets? In accordance with the Kepler's Third Law, their motions and distances from the sun will rearrange themselves immediately, as a powerful factor influencing their revolution has disappeared. A similar effect would result if the motions of Jupiter were suddenly changed, enhanced or dampened. This mutual dependence is so strong that thanks to the observed discrepancies between the actual planetary motions and the calculated ones, the English astronomer Adams was able to predict the existence of Uranus purely by mathematical means. Not only he showed the existence of the new planet, but also pointed to the very place where this planet should be present. (Independently of Adams the French astronomer Leverrier calculated it similarly). Neptune was actually found later in a similar way. If instead of moving Jupiter we were to remove or change the motions of Mars, then the rearrangements of the planets would be different.

Kepler's harmonic law (the Third Law), to which this German astronomer came by studying harmonics (see his work *Harmonices Mundi*), can be applied not only to heavenly bodies, but also to atoms and molecules. If, for instance, we were to remove one molecule from ten others in a certain area, then those ten would immediately rearrange their motions accordingly. The whole Universe, both atomic and astronomical is ruled by this same law of the mutual dependence of the motions of bodies freely suspended in space.

Now the growth of a body, so long as it is not interfered with by some outside force, will follow this harmonic law. Matter will accumulate in relation to the forces acting in the interference pattern. This accumulated matter will also have a harmonically distributed field, which is the function of the vibration of material particles. Thus, for example, the liver will grow in the human body in harmony with its vibratory pattern and that of the surrounding organs, also with the surrounding wave-patterns of the environment. The molecules will accumulate in peaks and troughs in accordance with the ruling pattern.

Suppose now that into this field an alien impulse is introduced which vibrates in dissonance with the pattern of the liver and its natural law. It will produce a discord into this orchestrating field, and by its own vibrations will influence the molecular motions of the liver, producing a dampening effect by shifting their phase angle or by enhancing some components and nullifying others. A sort of forced vibration is imposed. If the liver is strong enough, that is, if its amplitude is of full strength and is not dampened by previous wrong impulses, then it will resist and finally force the new impulse (or the alien matter) to vibrate at the liver's rate and pattern. The alien pattern will only slightly dampen the vibration of the liver's molecules. If, however, the intrusive vibration should find in the liver's motions a resonating component and thus acquire some strength, then it will be able to impose its own vibrations on the liver A new molecular arrangement will occur, detrimental to the harmony of this organ, and hence to the whole body and its health or state of balance.

There are some reasons for believing that blood has a strong absorbing capacity for such vibration patterns. We shall return to this later. Thanks to its circulation it will spread such vibration throughout the organism. However, as other organs are not in resonance with patterns other than their own, they will not resonate to it in full strength. It may, nevertheless, easily happen, that one of the most distant parts of the body will be in resonance with one particular component of the spreading vibratory rate and wave-form, and so that this component will be enhanced. The amplitude will grow above the normal required for the harmonious (balance) health state; the heat will there increase and an inflammatory state will arise. If the phase of the damaging factor is not exactly in phase with the enhanced vibration of the organ concerned, beats will emerge in the form of pulses. Now the nervous tissues of this resonating organ have grown in harmony with the former pattern of the organ and its amplitude. If then this amplitude should suddenly grow above normal, and the pattern change, respective signals will impinge upon this nervous tissue, and will be sent to the brain. Such signals will most probably be perceived by the brain as pulsating pain. If, however, there is no phase difference between the wave-form of the forced vibration and the one natural to the organ, by steady enhancement of one of the components a steady impulse will be sent to the brain, and the pain instead of being felt as pulsation will be perceived as steady. Personally the writer believes that all pains are pulsating ones, but some of the pulses are so quick that they are felt as steady. This opinion is the result of purely theoretical considerations.

What will happen when the invader of the organism finds in one of the organs a component resonating more fully to its own vibration? From the theory of resonance, it is apparent that the amplitude of the resonating component should grow abnormally and tend to pass a critical point—we shall call it the strain breaking point—and the molecules will then break asunder and the tissue will start to decay. This process again is analogous to the singer singing into a glass. It will first respond by enhancing its vibration, but finally will break up entirely and splinter into pieces.

It may happen though that a tissue instead of decaying will grow, like the seed mentioned above, impelled by the vibration. Then an example of cancerous growth will occur. Just as matter, under a localised impulse, forms spreading fractures, so does a cancerous growth in some cases spread into its surroundings.

Returning to the decaying process, essentially it comes down to the processes involved in chemical decomposition.

Fever is actually a thermal process enhanced. In an organ, one of the components of its vibration pattern enhances the momentum of the molecules of that organ through resonance. The temperature grows as the momentum grows, that is the amplitude or intensity of the vibration. When the amplitude passes the strain breaking point the organ will start to decay. In order to prevent this, the circulating blood absorbs the heat due to the momentum of the molecules, and by spreading it throughout the whole organism increases the surface area of the radiation. Not only the localised amplitude of vibration, but its momentum is decentralised as much as possible, and so prevents decay, but it also permits the emission through radiation of the increased momentum of the body, simply because the surface area of the radiation is larger. The stronger the resonance which produces the increase in amplitude, the higher the fever. The heart beats quicker, the circulation of the blood is stronger, and the field radiation increases. It can be shown that all this is the mere function of increased heat. As a matter of fact, the pulsation of the heart is a function of the temperature, or more exactly a function of the general amplitude of the molecular vibration. We see here how, by the principle of resonance and wave theory, a great many things going on in the organism can be reasonably explained.

In problems involving fever it must be realised that it involves not only a simple enhancement of the linear momentum of molecules. It also must result in a change of the pattern of their momentum. This change of pattern, however, will depend on what component of the general pattern is resonating with the new, introduced vibration. Different invaders, having different wave-forms, will resonate differently with various components of the complex wave-form of any particular organ. Hence one would expect that in any particular illness, the thermal agitation of the fever would produce a different pattern in the Brownian movement of the blood. Theoretically every man according to his particular health and psychological state should have slight differences in the pattern of his blood and its thermal or Brownian movement.

An example will perhaps make this clearer. The reader may remember what has been said about the different rearrangements of planetary motions if Jupiter or Mars were to be removed from the planetary system. A similar reasoning can be applied this time to molecular motions in the problems of fever. In one particular illness some harmonic components of the general pattern are cancelled and others enhanced. In another illness different components are subjected to this. Hence in both cases a different rearrangement of motions will follow, analogous to the example of the heavenly bodies. We see how temperature is basically a gravitational phenomenon. Dr. Benham in his paper called "The Nature of Temperature," is definitely right in his general claim[22]. From the above it is concluded that there is no random element in thermal motion, though on a microscopic level, it may appear as such at first glance. The law of the mutual dependence of the motions of bodies freely suspended in space is fundamental here.

An organism's invader can by its new vibratory pattern not only enhance one of the components of the organism, but also cancel one that is vital to the organism's state of balance. This will happen when the respective frequencies are out of phase by $180°$. A standing wave will result which will nullify the action of this vital element, i.e., its vibration. No fever will result but pain or a lack of balance will be the effect.

As to the absorbing capacity of blood for different patterns of motions, you may remember what has been said about the sap of the plants and their crystallisation. It was presumed there that such sap should contain the vibratory patterns of the plant, and that it should therefore crystallize accordingly. Subsequent microscopic investigations seem to give experimental support in some cases. *Mutatis mutandis* the same principle can be applied to the functioning of blood. From its crystallisation pattern we should be able to recognise, at least in the most general way, what is actually going on in the organism. A sample of blood taken from the body during a particular illness, when vaporised and conveniently dried, should, thanks to its absorbing factor, crystallise in accordance with the vibratory pattern it actually contains. The so-called blood groups may find here their basic *physical* explanation. The actual crystallisation of blood, about which we know something from the interesting photographic slides obtained from the researches of Duranton and Countess Chrapowicka, may be a similar phenomenon. It must be emphasized however, that any changes in crystallisation should appear in the details and not in the fundamental crystalline network. Actually the so-called Laue method (with X-Rays) when applied to blood crystalline structures, should reveal most promising results[23]. The Duranton methods may also give further information. As all these researches are as yet in early stages, it is not yet time to make any definite statements, it is hoped that the foregoing theoretical discussion is logical enough to be accepted as a working hypothesis.

The writer has investigated microscopically the crystallisation patterns of catarrhal mucus in its different stages. It was observed that slight differences could be found in the crystalline structure when the catarrh passes through its varying phases. The patterns are beautiful, somewhat similar to leaves of fern or certain kinds of moss. In a different series of microscopic researches, the crystallisation of the albumin of eggs of domestic birds was examined. It showed, in accordance with the theoretical predictions, that each species of bird has a different pattern of crystallisation, although the generic pattern of birds is always preserved. When one has become conversant with these, it can then be immediately recognised to what kind of bird this particular albumin belongs. Such researches were carried out with a veterinary doctor, Mr. Briks, in 1949-50.

In the light of what was said above, the mechanism of the curative action of drugs and plants can be explained. A plant which has a similar pattern or wave-form to that of the particular invader, or illness, but out of phase by 180 degrees with it (i.e., the mirror picture of it), at the moment when it is properly introduced into the body, will automatically form a standing wave with the pattern of the illness, thus nullifying its activity. This also explains the Hahnemann principle of *Similia Similibus Curantur*. By "similarity " we mean the complete similarity of the waveform.

As to whether homoeopathic doses can be explained by the present theory, we as yet abstain from any opinion. The writer would like, however, to emphasize that he is not a medically trained man. Only the purely physical side is treated here. The last word as to medical matters we leave to those who are trained in this branch of science and art. A general working hypothesis is here only proposed from a purely physical standpoint.

Now a few words must be devoted to psychological problems, as we are dealing with the Psycho-Physical Law.

We all know from daily experience that our thought can move certain parts of our bodies. In other words our thought has a certain amount of force at its disposal. By that force we can change the position of at least a macroscopic amount of molecules of our bodies, as for instance a finger. We can move it. Can we, however, influence the very minute particles of our bodies, the molecules themselves, in the same way as we move an assemblage accumulated in, say, a finger? Can we change their amplitude of vibration? For example, influence their temperature, their rates of vibration or amplitude of vibration? We have no doubt as to the former, being able to move a finger, a leg, and so on, but the answer to the latter question is not evident. From previous considerations we know that influencing the rate of vibration and amplitude would have a definite result on our state of health. We could then change our health by thought. Some believe that autosuggestion is based, at least partly, on such possibilities. The difficulty is to observe changes so minute in comparison with the actual movement of a hand.

Analysing more closely some of the bodily functions, we can easily observe some changes in temperature produced by thought. It is particularly noticeable in sexual activity where certain thoughts change the flow of blood and temperature in the respective organs. Strong emotions are another example. It has also been demonstrated on several occasions that an intense thought, for instance thinking about a particular finger will raise its temperature, and this temperature change is measurable.

Let us consider the same problem from another angle in order to eliminate all possible objections. We definitely can send nervous impulses by thought to certain parts of our bodies. Such an impulse travelling along the nerves, will reach its end and will there change the molecular vibratory pattern. According to the components and kinds of the impulses sent, the vibratory pattern of the molecules will be transformed in the region of nerve endings. Every type of action must produce a similar kind of reaction. A great many nerve endings in a certain area will change the pattern of molecular vibration in that area. If such impulses become automatic and subconscious as a steady habit (acquired usually by a repetition of this action), this will definitely and consistently change the molecular vibration pattern. These patterns will permanently respond to particular impulses in a particular way. Physically we can define this as the ability of thought to change through the respective impulses issued from the brain, the actual directional (axial) freedom of vibration, in other words, the ability to change the crystalline network structure. As a matter of fact we do not see how one could move a hand without imparting well beforehand a certain motion to the molecules. Such motion must start from smaller groups and proceed to larger ones. We know that this is what actually happens.

From the study of psychology it is known that a habit consists of subconscious impulses sent to different parts automatically. As we have said, it is acquired by long repetition of the same action. The physical mechanism consists in an efficient response of a particular tissue (or muscle, or whatever it may be) and of its molecules to successive impulses. It must therefore be accepted that a habit is related to an efficient rearrangement of molecular structural vibration in this tissue. Under such habitual impulses, the further growth of this tissue and its arrangement will be definitely and permanently influenced. The detailed regrouping and re-arrangement of molecules will be subject to habits. Thus the mental process influences growth.

In the absence of any thought interference with growth and its molecular arrangement, the body will grow then according to the law of harmonics. The chemical nature of molecules, their environment and their bonds, will influence growth according to the vibratory pattern governing this area. This pattern will arrange itself, as with the rearrangements of planetary bodies in harmony with their movements and fields. There would be no disharmony, no discord in such a body, organs, tissue etc. The musical field of such a body, as well as the body itself, would be a harmonious phenomenon. The field which is the function of our body's vibratory pattern would be beautifully and harmoniously distributed. The whole body can be compared to an orchestra, where each particular organ represents an instrument. Our thought is the conductor of this orchestra.

Now, the very moment that thought enters in, impulses are sent to different parts of the body, electrical signals sent through the nerves, and according to these impulses the molecules start to re-arrange themselves. This in turn affects the environment, and the transmitted radiation will accordingly arrange the surrounding field of the body. This explains how thought can influence the human field and the actual growth of the body. Permanent habits through their repeated impulses will influence the respective vibratory patterns of molecules, and the way they accumulate in the body. Thus the character of the man, his mental habits, will be definitely reflected in the body, in his way of moving, in his eyes, his face, hands, and so on. Even his way of working will be affected. Thought will affect the growth of the details in the general shape of the body, will carve its lines there. This is the reason why we can guess the general lines of a man's character from the way he walks, from his face and his palms. Thought actually influences the whole reactive system of molecular vibration. The whole body is formed according to the thoughts and habits animating it. What we call soul is the preponderating factor, the essential force which influences the whole and every part of it.

Human thoughts can be either in complete accordance with the natural law of harmonics and the general pattern of the human being, the generic pattern of its vibration, or in disharmony with them. In the first case the body will develop harmoniously, and its field will then represent a glorious harmony, containing no impurities and no dampening effects. In the second case, the very moment that thought develops, impulses are produced which are in complete or partial contradiction with the law of harmony. The proportions of the vibrations produced by dissonant impulses will not fit into the generic human pattern of vibrations, or into the individual pattern of the man. A human field of this kind will be full of discords and dissonances.

Evil thoughts will create wave forms which will contradict the law upon which human nature has grown; will dampen the generic and individual pattern of the human being; will affect the balance; will spoil the perfect resonance. Therefore— speaking in terms of wireless circuits—a part of his energy will be released and go back to the *Generator*. The energy loss will weaken health and introduce into the body the stamp of illness and decay, which finally will result in death.

From the study of theology we know that what we call a sin is nothing else than a violation of the law of nature, i.e., law of harmony. We thus have here a partial explanation of the mechanism of sin and its natural, physical side. There are other sides as well, but they will not be discussed here. Anyway sin, or any evil thought, which is not in agreement with the law of nature, will be reflected in the body and in its field, and will appear as a dampening effect upon the living force. The strength of the individual to resist it is weakened, and decay sets in. Evil is the first step and the very root of destruction and death. As St. Paul says, "The wages of sin is death".

We have had a glimpse into the realm of natural theology. We have seen how natural philosophy, the world of science, does not contradict, but, on the contrary, supports the beauty of the teaching of Christ.

To finish, we would like to say that the Creator, who is perfect beauty in Himself, that is, in perfect proportion, must be reflected in His Creation. Anything which violates this law of harmony is called a sin. It is a dissonance in the harmony of the spheres and the beautiful concerto of the Universe. It is in contradiction with Beauty, and therefore also with Goodness and Truth.

15

THE PATTERN OF TELEPATHIC COMMUNICATION[1]

I t is a real pleasure to be able to speak on such a vital and fascinating subject as the transmission of thoughts. Initially, it is necessary to give an outline of basic, scientific facts upon which such communication might be based. In order to understand the phenomenon properly we must recall the theory of fields, the only concept in physics which is known to act at a distance. Presumably you are familiar with the many different fields in physics which include the gravitational field that acts between the sun and the planets, magnetic and electric fields.

When talking about telepathy, I am not only thinking about the transference of thoughts between human beings but also communication with plants and between them, with animals and even with the so-called dead objects. Research in this field is really stupendous. A few months ago an American gentleman, who is writing a book on communication with plants, showed me papers written on this subject in the U.S.A., Italy, Switzerland and other countries. Even in some universities in this country there is a lot of intensive research going on, although apparently it is being done very quietly. For communication with plants a lie detector is often used. There is no doubt now that plants do respond to human thoughts and emotions. As early as 1938 at one of the Polish technical universities experiments were being done very successfully with little animals such as Paramecium[2].

Is there any possible explanation for such phenomena? For a very long time research was carried out on the assumption that there must be a peculiar kind of radiation of an unknown nature. Mitogenetic radiation was suggested by Gurwitsch[3], ultra violet radiation by Cazamalli, and others have been proposed. The question arises, whether there is any field of radiation known to us now which could explain at least some of these facts without resorting to some unknown factor. We do not intend to deny such a possibility, but it seems reasonable to start by looking for some simpler and well known facts. We know for certain that animals, plants and other objects as well as humans emit at least three different kinds of radiation. Firstly heat, and hence infrared radiation; then sound, due to the temperature and Brownian movement of molecules in the body and finally electrical potential. Doctors use sound with their stethoscopes. Electrical potential has been very thoroughly explored by cardiograms, encephalograms and finally by Professor Burr, Dr. Northrup and their associates at Yale University. Many scientific papers were published by these people. Proof of the electric field is no longer needed.

Now it is clear that, as this radiation is the function of biological metabolism, it carries with it, as any radiation does, all information about any biological changes. Those are in turn the results of emotions and, in human beings, of thoughts. The conclusion is obvious, that information about thoughts is contained in those fields too. But it is a question of properly interpreting such signals.

Now, these fields may be called Secondary Fields as they are the result of biological functioning or, in dead things, of Brownian movement.

The Yale researchers described these fields as L and T fields. L stands for life and T for thought. The L field was well described by Professor H. Burr in his book: *Blueprint for Immortality* published just under a year ago. Professor Burr's first paper on fields, "Electrodynamic Theory of Life" was published in 1935[4].

To illustrate this, imagine looking at an atom from, for example, a hand. For the sake of convenience let us accept the Bohr model of the atom, magnified so that the nucleus is the size of an apple. Where would the next atom be? Between 1,000 to 2,000 miles away! Looking upon our bodies on this scale, we would see a vast universe containing many millions of trillions of atoms forming billions of galaxies. If the nuclei of these atoms were shining, as they are centres of energy, we would confront a vast, celestial, starry sky of unimaginable spaces. So you see, our body, of which we have only a statistical perception when using our senses, is actually a great void with little centres of energy in the forms of atoms, dispersed at enormous distances. One biological cell contains many millions of galaxies of atoms. What makes these atoms work organically as a unity, like in a biological cell? Something must make them cohere together, organize them, and make them work towards one goal. This void manifests itself as an electrical potential but behind this there must exist something which has been named the L field, the field of life.

When one of us moves a finger for example, what happens? Billions of galactic systems of atoms are being shifted from one place to another. What a noise! However, this illustration immediately shows us the power of thought over matter. It is the T field which moves atoms using the L field's vast centres of energy.

Behind these L and T fields there must still be something which organizes the atoms into an organic unity. It is called the Organizing Field. Some have called it *soul*, but Organizing Field seems to explain its function better.[5] Obviously, since it organizes matter it is independent of it, existing on a totally different, 'immaterial' level.

About two years ago an English scientist, Michael Watson, found that this vast space of inter-atomic void is filled with a fourth state of water. Water is solid as ice, liquid as water, gas as vapour, and then it has the ability to transform itself into the next stage, hitherto unknown, which is called the fourth state. It is no longer the same water. Known atomic models must be totally dismissed. It is something quite new and can now be photographed. It seems to be the same as Prana of Eastern religions, and what ancient Jewish traditions named Avir. The ancient Chinese also speak about the same sort of water[6]. Watson also found a fifth state of water which is pure radiation, a sort of luminescence. The fourth state of water responds to thought, the fifth manipulates the fourth. The implications of this discovery are immense. The Jewish tradition calls the fifth state of water Quaf in Hebrew. With this discovery incomprehensible references to water collected from both the Old and New Testaments fall into place: why water is used in Baptism, or the Water of Life that Christ spoke of when talking to the Samaritan woman. The meaning behind the symbol comes alive and it all starts to make sense. Astronomical space seems to be filled with the fourth state of water. The same applies to spaces between atoms. When its balance is upset by thought it becomes converted into vapour, then water. The same thing is repeatedly spoken about by the Chinese sages when they speak of the circulation of light which is essential to their mediation for expanding spiritual life; when the circulation stops there is no spiritual development. We may then understand why our bodies are 80-

90% water. It is strange that these states of water were discovered at the start of the Aquarian Age. Actually it seems that what Aristotle called *Materia Prima* is just this fourth state of water, responsive to thought. It is obvious that, when we move a finger, our thoughts influence the L field and then the body, because thought can imprint itself onto this state of water and produce effects such as tensions or patterns and thus transmit information. The T field has a tremendous power over the L field and, through it, on the body. The power of mind over matter may then be comprehended to a certain extent. It seems that the L field— the fourth state of water—would correspond to the concept of Prana mentioned by the sages of old in Sanskrit writings and later in the Far East. The fifth state of water however, being again something totally different from Prana, could correspond to the concept of Sanctifying Grace mentioned in theological treatises, brought into being by the *potentia obedientalis*, obedience to God's power from the human essence. This is pure radiation. We might suppose that a sixth and seventh state of water exist but we have no proof of it yet.

Let us return to the concept of the Secondary Fields mentioned earlier, heat, or infra-red radiation, electrical potential and sound. Their radiations are of a very short wavelength as they arise from the biological system and its changes. As with any other radiation, they must carry all the information about the changes in the body. Thus, the medicine of the future will be much more concerned with changes in the field instead of exploring, as it does now, the body itself. It is much easier to explore the field than the interior of the body. By projecting these fields on a cathode ray tube, all the necessary information may be obtained, long before the patient feels any pain, because these fields must be very strong in order to pass through the patient's threshold of awareness. Such medicine would be preventative; the complicated harmful signals would be fed into a computer, which would calculate the kind of signals to be fed back into the patient in order to reach a balance, and affect a cure.

This is actually what *we* do when we use our hands for healing. We pick up these signals with the central nervous system and feed the required information to our own computer, the subconscious brain. The brain sends necessary signals via the peripheral nervous system to the hands. Then the healer's field affects the patient's field, bringing about the required balance.

Now this balance is characterized by proper feedback. We know from physiology that living biological cells use feedback if they are to function properly. It is comparable to the circulation of the sap in plants, from the stem to the roots and back to the stem. In our case this concerns radiation or the transmission of radiation. Suppose that a certain pattern of radiation emitted by the liver does not return in its required quantity and quality to the body and to the liver; gradually the liver will suffer a dysfunction, and eventually the body becomes ill. A healing hand introduced into the field simply corrects the feedback to its normal state and restores the balance.

To understand the mechanics of this process, we have to realize that the phenomenon of resonance is the essential part of the healing process, or telepathic transmission. The human body is extremely sensitive in picking up different, complex signals of both Primary and Secondary fields. The Primary field, being the organizing one in the material world, is on a totally different level, so time and space do not play any part in it. In the Secondary Field, the Infra-Red and Electromagnetic Fields travel with the speed of light, 186,000 miles a second. Therefore, in 1/8 of a second, roughly speaking, the Electromagnetic Field circles the world and comes back to the transmitting body, whereas heat, which is the infra-red radiation has the ability to travel along the surface of the earth. It is therefore easy to grasp that, because our fields cover the whole earthly globe in 1/8 of a second, they are everywhere, and to tune into them is no mystery. As to communication in interstellar space, here the Primary Field can be of great assistance.

Now how does the so-called "tuning in" take place? All radionics practitioners, dowsers and the like know well that in order to be in resonance with a patient or another human being we have to have in hand what is called a Witness. Hair, a blood spot, a photograph or a fingerprint give us a possibility to be in touch with the owner of the Witness. What does this mean? We know that every one of us is a unique person with a unique pattern of proportions both physical and psychological. Hence the field and also the Witness represent this unique quality. By tuning into the wave form of this unique pattern we resonate with these proportions only, and all others are eliminated. Such tuning in is a special ability and must be developed by proper training. In telepathy the subject at the receiving end must tune into the transmitting subject with his mind, training himself to resonate to his unique field pattern, and in addition, to interpret the signal in that pattern into a known language.

Do we have such an ability? A very simple experience from every day life suggests that we do. If every one in the room were to talk simultaneously, in order to hear one person, we tune in by eliminating from our awareness all other sounds. Actually, we hear everyone, but our awareness is sensitized at that moment to one talker only whether in the vicinity or far away. We say that we focus our attention on this particular set of sonic proportions and therefore we hear only this person, these sounds or that music. The same applies to our vision; we see the entire picture which falls into our visual range, but we can also focus on a part of it. We can look and see nothing, but we can also look and see; or we can look, see and perceive. We actually focus our awareness on specific signals. We have trained our awareness to focus on signals arriving from our normal senses which reach our computer brain. But have we trained ourselves to pick up signals coming from our Secondary Fields? Because they contain short wavelength radiation they behave like radar. Part of our radiation is absorbed by our environment, a part is refracted and goes into space, but part of it is reflected and comes back to us bringing information. Unfortunately, we have done everything possible not be aware of these signals. Our whole culture is based on rationalisation and we have killed our intuition and perception of a radar-like nature based on this sort of radiation.

The aerial for this is our hair, which is known to be the best conductor, apart from spider web, for sound. With its enormous dielectric capacity hair is sensitive both to the electric field and to the infra red. If you study the histological structure of the hair you will find that the bulb of the human hair is wonderfully rich in nerves; three to five nervous tips are connected to the bulb. What are they for? Nature never does things without purpose. These nerves are there to pick up signals and transmit them to the central nervous system. However, we have blocked our awareness of these signals and hence we do not know of them.

It is amazing how on television programmes, people from the general public are chosen in order to try to prove or disprove telepathy. It is just as if I would call a number of people off the street and ask them to play a piano. If they stated that they did not know how to play, then the conclusion would be that the piano is not playable! Experiments done in many countries on plants have shown unmistakably that plants have wonderful telepathic abilities. Many papers have been published already about it.[7] Distance does not come into this communication. It is known that if you have a plant about which you really care and you travel a long distance from it, even to the other side of the globe, the very moment you are in danger the plant shows its anxiety as an electrical impulse, registered if the plant is connected by an electrode to an amplifier and a polygraph.

From what has been related here we know that the fourth state of water is responsive to the T field, that is, to thoughts. Now the L field (the fourth state of water or Prana) fills all spaces between the atoms of the air, earth, and human bodies. By thought we influence the L field, which in turn influences the atomic vibrations and, also molecular vibrations so that they can reach the fabulous computer of the human brain. If we train ourselves properly, our awareness is immediately informed. We had to train ourselves to write and read and we have to do the same with our inner senses. Then and only then shall we be able to pick up signals, be aware of them and interpret them properly into an intelligible form of message. Courses on how to do it are actually run by the Wrekin Trust in this country. People are amazed that in one weekend they can learn so much. However, at the same time we must develop our spiritual life, otherwise we expose ourselves to the danger of landing up in a lunatic asylum.

We can discover that our awareness is not limited by space and time by conducting a very simple experiment with ourselves. All of us know well that we can observe ourselves. One can observe one's anger, jealousy, joy and so on. You can watch yourself being angry or frustrated or joyful and you can analyse what you are like when you are angry or jealous, and so on. What does this mean? It means that you can withdraw in your mind to what we call *The Observer* and observe your own emotions, your thoughts and your body. Try to examine your day every evening for, say, a week, watching yourself being in the body, looking at yourself as a movie actor looks at himself on the screen. After a short period of time you will notice that your Observer can look upon your body moving in space and being subject to time: hours, morning, noon and evening. Your Observer is not concerned with such trivialities, since it is not in time or space. Only your body is subject to these factors. Then you will swiftly find out that actually you are much more the Observer, whereas the body is your instrument which your own self manipulates. The Observer is your real self and it does not live in space and time but outside it You can actually observe one whole hour, one day, or a hundred years at one go. One looks upon time and space. In your imagination, try to go to your own room wherever it is whilst you are now here. Can you see it? Yes, you can; you can be in the room, or embrace the whole room. Using your imagination, go into space and look upon the earthly globe; in one glance you can embrace it.

Here it is important to distinguish between imagination and fantasy. After Kierkegaard, fantasy is what we create in our inner vision and has no reality in the objective world, but imagination is the inner or third eye, which has the power to create what we perceive objectively. Because we have never been trained to distinguish between the two, we mix them up and think that they are synonymous expressions whereas they refer to two definite, separate faculties. If you train yourself to separate them, and the method of training is simple, you can easily see at a distance or become clairvoyant. May I ask how you were able to see, perhaps in your dreams, events which took place a few days later? Using your eyes? You were fast asleep at the time. Perhaps you saw something two years in advance, or a place which you visited a month later and which you instantly recognized though you'd never been there before. If you dig into your memory you will find that you were actually there in a dream. You used your Observer, your third eye. This is the work of your imagination and not your fantasy, which is a creative force, although if it mixes with imagination you do not know whether you actually see truth or just fantasy.

Here perhaps you can see the importance of your Observer. After a while you will find that you have quite unnecessarily identified yourself with the body, and, further, you will find that you are actually *not in the body, but the body is in you.* Your Observer is a very large something which is actually coextensive to the whole universe. Thus you are really created in the likeness and similarity of God. But because you have limited yourself to the perimeter of your skin, you see yourself as merely a speck in a vast space. The very moment you withdraw to your Observer, your real self, then and only then can you see yourself as a giant and can consider your body merely as a transformer of your field, just like a transistor set, is a transformer of a BBC transmission. Can you now see what you actually are? And, mind you, this is only the first step. You are actually much more than this.

This is only a very brief statement in order to give you a clearer picture of how telepathy can be rationally explained and is actually a fact. There is much more to it than meets the eye. It has nothing to do with so-called extrasensory perception. There are many inner *senses* which we have never developed. In fact we have done everything possible to kill them inside ourselves by blocking our awareness of them or laughing at them, as so many so-called scientists do, who have not even a clue as to what they are talking about. To give you another instance. In art you have visual art—painting, sculpture and architecture. Then there is an art for the auditory senses: music and speech. There is also an art for smell as well as for taste, but what sort of art do we have for our tactile sense? Perhaps we have killed that art, of "being in touch" via our radar-like field perception. Have you ever tried to touch an object at a distance through this kind of Secondary Field radiation, and interpret the signals received? Again, if you train yourself in it—and this is not very difficult, a weekend suffices—you will find that a new world has opened up to you. How it works has been described above. Of course, if we have blocked our awareness against such signals we shall never pick them up. We block ourselves by simply not believing that this is possible. I have trained some youngsters during a weekend and within twenty minutes some of them, while blindfolded, recognize signals from bracken, gorse, or ivy.

When Christ was asked what is the greatest commandment in the Law, He answered, the Commandment Of Love. It is here that He gives us a hint because this commandment starts with the words: "Hear, O Israel, the Lord Our God is one God..." The first condition to pick up signals is to listen and then to hear. It boils down to the phenomenon of resonance. Love is just resonance, resonance to a field. With love one listens and develops an awareness of the environment. A special meditation technique has been devised called the E.M.T. (Environmental Meditation Technique) in order to develop such awareness[8]. Actually it is a calamity that all methods of meditation, at least the ones that I have come across, tacitly assume that we are in the body, limited by our skins, instead of realizing that the body is in us. And this attitude makes a great difference concerning the development of awareness for the very simple reason that once you are conscious that your field—your Observer—is actually coextensive with the whole universe then you have all the signals at hand and only need to pick out the ones you want to be aware of. However, you know that the rest are at your disposal the very moment you turn your focussing power on them. You are no longer limited; expansion takes place, and by listening, by this *shema* as it is called in Hebrew, you begin to love, for through listening and hearing His love, He starts to operate in you. Love always opens the gate to listening and hearing and eventually leads to harkening, which means to understand the message deeply. Let me explain this. By listening you only pick up the mere signals. It is exactly the same as if someone were to send you a book written, for example, in Arabic or Turkish. You see the signs, you know that there is something there because the signals are coming to your eye, but you are not able to read it. This is the first sensitivity, the listening. The second conception of *shema* is hearing. The signals are picked up and you know how to interpret them superficially. When reading a book you understand the story but the actual message is missed. The third concept is the harkening. You read the book, pick up the signals and also go into it deeply, just like reading and understanding the signals of nature.

Present day physics limits itself to the surface, and is analogous to sending someone a book and asking them to read it and give an opinion of it, only to receive the reply that the paper is made out of such and such chemicals, the letters from grease, with so many circular and so many straight letters and so on, which is quite interesting but leaves the meaning of the book still not understood. This is what is meant by listening, hearing and harkening, or perhaps looking, seeing and perceiving. In the case of our book the physicist has limited himself to its surface. Nature is a great book written to us in an unknown language, and *shema* means just learning the actual language and gradually understanding or harkening to the message. This is all implied in so-called E.M.T. Now this is just what radionics tries to do; it tries to pick up signals and expand our awareness of them through instrumental means, or through the supreme instrument we have: our body and, specifically, our hands. One can pick up signals by training not only the hands but the whole body. Quite a lot of information on this subject is found in Rudolf Steiner's book, *Knowledge of the Higher Worlds* Another one is by Jane Roberts', *How to Develop the Third Eye* and there are many others which you know probably better than I.

Obviously, it is impossible to cram into one hour's talk even the essential information. However, we can assure you that all this is well grounded and I do hope you can at least see that it has a reasonable basis. For example, in distant healing medical doctors are sometimes amazed at the results but because they have not been informed of the theory of fields they do not understand it. However, once you have grasped the concept of fields and radiation, then the whole thing starts to appear as a reasonable proposition. It is pure physics or perhaps it may be better described as psycho-physics. Anybody can be trained to open their inner senses which up until now have been latent and silent. After a while you will find new worlds open to you, new possibilities, new expansion of awareness and an inner experience which words cannot express. We have been so completely mesmerized by our lower senses, eyes, ears and so on, that *we* have neglected the inner ones. But we know well that these outer senses so often mislead us, whereas the inner ones are many times more accurate.

Once you have grasped these principles we can go into telepathy. You will find that by training yourself, it is very easy to communicate with rocks, plants and animals. However people are really hard nuts to crack because they are so absorbed by their own concepts and way of thinking, so brain-washed that they hardly ever listen let alone hear. I am talking not only about other people but also about myself. The arrogance with which we are imbued is quite incredible. As Steiner puts it so rightly, arrogance and impatience are the main obstacles to developing our inner senses. Hence, we are not able to hear signals from others, and therefore telepathic communication is cut off. In order to communicate you have to listen. Could you communicate with anyone if the other side would not listen? Well, the same applies to telepathy. You can see, I hope, the connections. The biophysical base is always in the field's resonance, whereas the resonance is not in the transmitting part, but is mainly at the receiving end which must be perceptive. *Shema is essential.* The trouble with us is that we do not want to hear or even listen. Let us train our inner ears to hear, and then telepathy will not be a mystery but an everyday experience. No proof shall be needed.

16

PLAYING YOUR
MUSIC — A DIALOG

This dialog took place at the Westbank healing centre, November 1968. Participants are not identified and are referred to throughout the text as "Questioner".

The recording starts in mid-discussion. Andrew was answering a question about a vision of higher worlds. How does such a vision change one's life? What happens afterward?

AG: Something to think about. You know the physical world is important. You love it, but you're not attached to it. Because you see the new one, and the next one, that this is this and this is that. And strange enough, when you go really far then you come back to the physical world, but you see it as totally different.

Questioner: So, you come back here?

AG: Yes. You are back again in this world but not in it. You enjoy this world; that's a sort of reincarnation but you see it from a different angle, because you have progressed in your music. I don't know if you are a musician. You start with a theme, and you develop that theme in one key and then you go to the next key. One music, three different tunes in three different keys. Not linked to one another but these three tunes are playing together. You can listen to one tune and be absolutely satisfied, to the second and be satisfied and third as well; and the three tunes together play a harmony. It's a development. You go to the next key, then the next and then eventually you return to the first key. It's the general composition of a musical work. Well it's exactly the same, because music is a symbolic representation of what is going on in the psycho-physical world. You develop this theme and then you go on and on. And sometimes you come back to the dominant but in a different way. You have the first keyboard, and then the next keyboard on an organ, and then the next in totally different surroundings. You go in a spiral, come back to the same place but over it, the same curve but one degree higher and then one degree higher. Then somehow you collect the three themes together to form an inexpressible harmony.

Questioner: What about those people you just mentioned who never learned to play the piano at this party? Is this what reincarnation is? Are there other parties that they go to?

AG: No, they roam about the world not knowing they are dead. I have quite a lot of experience with this. They consider themselves as being dead. Or not conscious and being in the coffin which is obviously not true because you leave your cocoon and fly out like a butterfly. They don't know that, so they go around the world shouting to people but nobody listens to them. So they are enraged.

Questioner: But they're not going to do this ad infinitum because surely they eventually learn something, and they learn to play their piano...

AG: Or they fall into a certain state where they cannot get out, and that is a terrible state for them. And then somebody comes from outside and cuts their bonds. But that's a totally different thing. I would have to devote a whole lecture on it.

Questioner: What about suffering? Is it induced by the subconscious?

AG: It's from the clash of your will which is wrongly informed by your imagination, or led by your imagination, with your own physical development. Psycho-physical development. Your imagination clashes with it and produces a signal that tells you that something is wrong; and this is pain. It may be mental pain or physical pain. Which reminds me, you won't find one place in the gospels where God tells you that you have to add pains to your everyday experience. He says that you have to meet the pains but never add to them. So don't carry out any mortification in order to do mortification because it's nonsense. It's against the teachings of Christ. You meet whatever happens in your life with joy and acceptance and never escape it. And then you'll find how to suffer; if you are loving. That the secret. If you are loving, the suffering vanishes. The cloud is gone.

I'll tell you of an experience I had. I went to a doctor who was doing some research on a girl, in his laboratory. There was an ultraviolet light there, and I was careless enough to look into that light for a short moment. I remembered that you can lose your eyesight if you look into it, but nothing happened. I went home and went to sleep. In the night I woke up with fantastic eye pain. I opened my eyes, lit a light and only saw a faint appearance of light. Nothing else. And I understood that I'm losing my sight. That I shall never see again. And from the bottom of my heart I said, "Thank God for that. I shall open my eyes in the next world." But for the sake of eliminating the pain I went to the bathroom, washed my eyes and went to sleep, feeling joyful. I woke up in the morning, still with the pain but seeing things perfectly. It's a device in our organism. If you meet something with joy, the organism immediately sets that device in motion to mend the difficulty in the physical world.

Questioner: Your own physical world? That was something that happened inside you. Surely there are things outside you too that can be mended.

AG: Yes, but this time it was with my eyes, my eyesight. And I accepted it with terrific joy. And because of that I eliminated the progression of the loss of eyesight. I got it back, and I realized that it is necessary for me to see this world in order to comprehend others. But that is the secret of meeting our crosses with joy and not with sorrow, such as, "Oh what a poor boy I am!" A masochistic sort of thing. That's no good. When it's not masochistic, and you say, "Great, I will have it." And you fix your attention on something totally different, you are not bothered by this. If you are bothered, then you object to it. If you fix your attention on something different, then you are not obstructing, not blocking the repair.

Questioner: That seems like detachment. How do you explain it?

AG: It's difficult to explain. You may have to experience the pain. You see, pain is only given to you to teach you something. Any illness I've had, I knew was there to teach me something. And I try hard to find out what, and when I found out, immediately the illness disappeared.

Questioner: What you call the secondary plane, is it the same as the sub-conscious?

AG: Obviously you have two sides, the unconscious and the overconscious, and the conscious. There are three quasi-personalities. And if you talk to yourself, it's not the first sign of insanity. Because the conscious talks to the subconscious and to the overconscious in order to communicate with them in a physical way. And strange enough you have to talk about it. I talk to plants and then they grow. You can be silent with them, and love them, but they will not grow as much as if you talk to them.

Questioner: Why is that? Is there something in the vibration of the voice?

AG: In the vibration of the voice, yes. It's your expression, something I use when I preach. You have to preach from the bottom of your heart which means your absolute self, and then you find that the intonation of the words, the music of the speech as such, has a magical influence on the audience, somehow or other. You have the audience and they can hear A B C D....X Y Z and so on. It's just like playing a harp, many sounds that form a unity. You start to play the strings and then all the strings play together, musically, because you have been playing very nicely. Because playing your harp together, as a group, gave you much pleasure. I think I explained that to Bruce. It is his way to gather you together, as a coherent group, playing what you have been instructed, bringing your experiences to the group. Therefore you produce an instrument to play on.

If you have a piano and you don't play the piano, the piano deteriorates. You have to play on it, and then you start to grow. But it depends on how you play it. The piano will deteriorate if you play it wrongly, and it improves if you play it right. The art is not just to play the keyboard but play with a sensitive touch of your fingers. The whole art is in striking the keyboard so that your fingers touch the strings with harmony. As you play with greater speed, you have to be able to play so that each finger has a different touch. And not until then are you a master. You have a mood, and the piano plays your mood, exactly what you want. For me it's a drug like LSD. I haven't touched the piano for twenty five years, because I would just drop everything and play. I listen to music with a tape recorder but I can't play. I play on other instruments now in my parish, but I can't touch the piano because I would drop everything if I started to play it. It's like magic.

Questioner: Can you communicate through the piano?

AG: Oh yes, because I studied it. And strange enough if anybody whispers when I play, I stop. I'm like Liszt when the Tsar started to talk. He stood up and walked out. Back in 1940/41 when I played, if somebody talked it stopped me.

Questioner: Would you not say perhaps that what you say, that you can't touch the piano because then you would drop everything, is only true as you see it now and has maybe become a truth for you because you've said it so often that it is now in your subconscious?

AG: No, it would take eight hours a day.

Questioner: What I'm saying is could you not influence your subconscious that says, you can't play the piano.

AG: To play the piano you have to practice.

Questioner: I mean, realize that you could play the piano without dropping everything else.

AG: It's no good playing the piano without practising. Four hours to eight hours a day. And I cannot afford four hours a day. I would not be able to talk to you. So I have to drop it. And as with smoking, or alcoholism or a drug addiction, you start and you cannot stop. I can't explain what an effort it was for me to stop. But I did. I love to play and if I had time I should sit down and play again.

Questioner: What I was trying to stay. The subconscious influences you. Can you influence your subconscious? I detest apples. I don't like apples, and if I say it often enough...

AG: Of yes. If you want to stop smoking, the best way is to tell yourself that you don't like smoking, and after a while you really don't like smoking and so you stop. But it's not a question of will power but of imagination.

Questioner: I know. I've given up hundreds of times.

AG: If you give up, you start again. But if you persuade yourself that you don't like it then you don't want to smoke at all.

Questioner: Can you use that knowledge to advance along the spiritual path?

AG: Oh yes. By visualizing that you have achieved the goal. You set yourself a goal and then you say, 'Of course I will achieve it.' So you go on and on and on, and you go you go higher and higher. What I told you today is, as I said to Malcolm, is the first step. I didn't tell you the next step or the next step because you wouldn't understand.

Questioner: What then is the goal at this stage? I would think that the goal would just be to be at one.

AG: Yes. You have to practice LLT, Light-Love Technique. And then knowledge comes automatically to you. Like when you go to a certain meeting, and you meet somebody or you take a book and suddenly you know something. It just comes in an easy way. 'English without tears.' It probably feels like that. Somebody learns English without a big effort. It happens that way, without tears. LLT works by itself. You should not make a big effort. If you make a big effort you get the opposite effect. It comes easily. Through love. You love and therefore you do it. The more you do, the more you love, and the more you love the more you do. I would love for instance instead of practicing the piano, to tune in with my imagination to the field say, of Chopin or Liszt. Tune in so that I will not play but Liszt will play for me. I'll have a fantastic technique without practicing. And I know that I shall come to that, but for now I have to go through the dark ages. Then, I shall not need to practice.

Questioner: Somebody is doing that right now.

AG: Yes, Rosemary Brown. Well, she's not playing; she's composing, giving out compositions. But it's not a question of composition. I want to play. There was a man who didn't have a clue how to play. They told him simply, "Sonata in D by Beethoven", and he said, "Oh yes." And he played the sonata. He never knew it, never knew about Beethoven.

Questioner: You've actually seen him?

AG: No, but I know about him from a friend of mine who was present. The pianist was a very simple person who didn't have clue how to play.

Questioner: Didn't he sit facing north?

AG: Tuning in he faced north for some reason which I couldn't decipher. But I'm quite sure that he could play. If you tune into the field you suddenly acquire the agility Chopin had when he was here. A sort of reincarnation of Chopin, so that Chopin will play for you. Someone looking on me will see Chopin because I will transform my face into Chopin's. I would still preserve my own face, but it would have his expression. It's as I was talking to you today. It wasn't me. I'm a simple channel. Provided I am nothing. The more I'm nothing, the better I am a channel for something else. The same thing is with the piano. If I am aware of myself, I am aware of my ten fingers which cannot properly touch the piano keyboard. So as long as I have this feeling I can't play quickly. When I lose this feeling I play like an accomplished pianist. And that's the energy way of living. I would love for instance to tune into a book so that I could comprehend the book immediately; and not only the book but the actual mind of the writer. Then there's no need to read the book. If you put your hand around a book you will see a certain beam with a certain direction. Through this direction you go in and then you'll know all about the book. And that will be the best way of teaching children because they spend the best years of their lives on the school bench, which is a waste of time.

In the Kingdom, you're already young. You'll pass from one stage to another, one level to another and you disintegrate and then integrate elsewhere. Going then through different levels you come back. For people here it will be 500 years. For you it may be seconds. Or vice versa. You're walking through the star dust, a simple thing provided you are nothing. He is everything. I have to diminish and he has to grow. The words of St. John. It's always selfishness which is the obstacle. The self, awareness of myself, that I shall show something to somebody, so that they will admire Me. And then, it's an obstacle. Right now you admire me and I'm very happy about it. It is not a lack of humility because I know that you love Him through me. Well, fair enough; He should be admired. Go ahead, don't worry about it. I am not the target. I don't think of it and so I'm happy. If I were to take it to myself I would be happy and you wouldn't stand me. He has to grow and I have to diminish. Provided you love, love as a giving love. The biggest bore in life is to be concerned with yourself. There are so many interesting things around yourself, and they somehow come back to you.

Questioner: Is it possible to have some sort of harmony with a machine?

AG: Oh it's known that a machine will work with one person and not with another.

Questioner: Because I find that if I talk to my sewing machine it perks up. This has got me fairly frightened.

AG: It's all the same, a sewing machine, aircraft or car. Have you ever come across a course called "A Course of Living Faith"? A new branch of psychology called nexology brought out twenty lessons on the "Living Faith" about beliefs. Any sort of beliefs. It's not necessary to believe in God. In the second lesson, I think, they talk about how you can talk to a machine and improve the machine. One of the founders gave an example of driving a car from California to New York. The car badly needed repair at a garage. He started off, and during the first two hundred miles he was talking to the car. The car came to New York in a much better condition than it started with. Then he started to think about how a set of beliefs can influence a car. A sewing machine is a living being. A car has a personality. If you've had many cars during your life you'll know that each car has a different personality. One is diligent and one is lazy. One is vicious and one is obstructive. They each have their own personality and taste, and you have to talk to them to find out what it is. Sometimes with your hand and you can foresee a danger, and so you avoid the danger; eliminate an accident. You come to the place of the accident to be, two minutes earlier or five seconds later. But somehow you have an intuition, and you slow down here and not there. You don't know why but you eliminate the danger.

Questioner: Do you find that this gets across to a congregation more easily than many other abstruse things? You know, I can imagine that at Attingham around New Year when Sir George has the young people's conference, that this is a concept that they would understand very readily.

AG: It would depend on what sort of views they have. I find the youth of today absolutely wonderful. I've never met such youngsters as today's. All of today's hippies or beatniks, they have such wonderful characters but they don't know where to go. Yesterday I was at a tea party and two youngsters came. After five minutes they were absolutely excited. Every one of them works hard; a wonderful bunch of people—called themselves Loonies. They took me for a Loony, so I'm all right. There was a boy among them with long hair, locks like you, and he asked me to treat something about him. So I sat down and started to wave my hand, and when I started, his hair stood up like this, following my hand. I hadn't touched him. George was passing by and said, "Goodness gracious what are you doing there?" I hadn't thought of it as peculiar. It shows that we are dealing with an electric field. But they're a wonderful bunch. They're constantly coming to me in Devon, when they pass by. There's a girl, four weeks on a course who has now gone on to India. A beautiful girl and so wise, though she's eighteen years of age. I took her to two of my groups and within ten minutes everybody was sitting around her, listening to her. That's the current youth; they have something to say. Yesterday two youngsters with long hair came in. Obviously their mothers didn't like their hair. And I said that hair is a natural aerial to pick up those peculiar fields. Sound especially. Hair is also the best conductor for static electricity and for heat. It picks up the field beautifully. And I said, "If I had my hair short I would be déclassé. I would not know what to do. Without my hair, my aerials, I don't feel right." So Johnny said to mummy, "See I told you." It's a good aerial I should say, provided you keep your hair in order and not every hair in another direction which some hippies are doing. Well that isn't an aerial.

Questioner: Too bad if you're bald.

AG: Bald is from too much energy. You're thinking too much, concentrating your energy in the head. Bald people are stuffed with too much energy.

Questioner: If you get bald when you're older, does that mean that you think more when you're older?

AG: No. Why do you think that energy accumulates more and more in the head? It's because the function of the circulatory system is off. It doesn't bring a new supply.

Questioner: So you should think less?

AG: No. You should radiate energy more. With your hands. As we grow older we absorb it more. Through selfishness you keep more to yourself. You have to be a perfect channel like any biological cell in the planet. You receive certain things, you give them out. And then you can absorb new forms. But if you receive and keep energy for yourself, for your self-enjoyment, thinking about how wonderful you are, then of course you do not radiate enough. You have to radiate it.

One day I said to myself, "what a magnificent person I am."

The plants told me, "Why don't you radiate your illness to the Earth?"

"Because I don't want to hurt you, to permeate the Earth with my illness. The pain is my pain. I don't want to communicate that."

"You're very mean," they said.

"Why? Isn't it for me to keep my pain to myself?"

"No. Certainly not. You are false; stuck in your own self, your sickness. You think, what a wonderful person you are, that you can keep your pains to yourself. You're stuck in yourself. You must remember that what we exhale you inhale. That what you exhale we inhale. So if you radiate your illness to us, it will give us pleasure and life. In exchange we'll give you our life."

You see, how conceit and selfishness make us assume a role of what a wonderful thing we are that we're keeping our suffering to ourselves. I was being selfish. Plants can feed you. Beautifully, as I've said before.

It's not just imagination. I believe that in the future we will eat much less, being fed by plants in exchange for giving them energy. They give us different forms of oxygen. They are not all the same. You use some to inhale and others not.

Illness often comes because the inner parts of the lungs are filled with certain patterns of electricity due to your selfishness, due to your point of view from a certain belief. You have certain patterns and not others. Because you are jealous, the particular pattern that you need for your liver will not reach your liver and your liver will deteriorate; because you are not supplying the right pattern. If you get rid of jealousy, the pattern returns and your liver comes back to normal.

Questioner: What you said about hair. Do you think that animals and plants are more sensitive than us, because they have many very small hairs?

AG: It's because they don't have blockages like we have. Prejudices. We have prides and prejudices and put up blockages against the flow of energy. When I have a patient I immediately start to send them light and love and he starts to breathe. The improved breathing immediately results in him being healed. And the breathing is usually connected with the sympathetic nervous system, which means a certain set of emotions. And these emotions are usually regulated by a certain set of beliefs. If I believe for instance that you are my enemy because three persons tell me that you are my enemy, then I will obviously develop a resentment toward you. That is a set of beliefs that produces emotion. Emotion has a terrific influence on our illnesses. Eighty percent of all our illnesses are due to negative emotions. Plants haven't got them. They are as they are, but we wear a mask. You want to appear better than you are. Everybody wears a mask. And when I said that we must find it out, I mean that we must find ourselves and be ourselves.

That's what youngsters want to be today. They drop all conventions. They want to appear as they are. They want to improve their own existence and therefore they are looking for guidance. Everybody condemns them. It's wrong. We have to give them a hand. I never saw such beautiful persons as youngsters today.

They want to pray but they cannot stand the conventional side of prayer: mumbling words that sound like rubbish. You go to church because you have to go, and then you say, "I am a good Christian because I go to church." Instead of going to church in expectation, because something is happening there, you're happy when you leave the church and say, "Thank God it's over." But it's due to the main actor in a dog's collar who doesn't know what he's doing. He doesn't understand group phenomenon or group prayer. You look around, say a prayer. The other actors are the audience in the great drama, but don't know what's going on. They go to church just to appear there. Nobody explained to them the group role in the drama. How it works. How to feel it, and how the group can influence the whole atmosphere of Earth and Space. They don't know. So they go to the church and leave it happy that they've finished with it. If you produce in the church a little spell, people will come in and say, "I don't know what happened there but it was quite nice. Quite pleasant." I've never been taught about group prayer. Nobody taught me; I had to work it out for myself. I still don't know very much about it. How to begin. People often come to the church and leave crying like mad even though they don't know what's going on or what I'm doing. Afterwards it hits them that something beautiful was going on.

Group prayer involves a certain technique of tuning into the group. Working together, linking up, you usually have to go above the heads of the group. Like having a hundred different strings, you play on them like a piano's strings. You go into a different world, and there comes the intonation of the words. You talk, and it's spoken payer. It's not a question of how you say it. If you say it to impress people you will fail miserably. You just talk from the bottom of your heart. You are just in touch with the others and they feel it. The fire lights and it increases and increases. The people in the church are one. Sitting here, you are also one because I am talking to you. I am talking from the bottom of my heart, and you're listening carefully.

Questioner: I have heard a top actor say in the same words almost exactly what you've been saying about a theatre audience.

AG: Yes, it's a special art. But he's actually acting. You cannot be a good actor unless you fit yourself into the role as such. Once you fit yourself into the role you are a perfect actor. But it means filling yourself so that you forget about being Andrew Glazewski. You are just a priest. You radiate to people, God and to all Creation. Then you introduce the people as priests because you are all priests, ordained as priests through confirmation and baptism. What is imprinted in your soul is the sacramental character, deputation of a divine code, deputation of radiation between Creation and God. What do you give Creation? Light and love. But you never thought of it. As that priest you give out light and love, and they can count on it. And once you fit yourself into that role, it works.

Questioner: Do you find that the congregation in your parish will accept this?

AG: They will accept it without knowing. The subconscious mind will work it out. I was giving a course in Swindon, a year ago. I went to the local chapel there with a congregation of a few people and some nuns. I said Mass as usual. The nuns said, "I never experienced the Mass like that, Father." It was exactly the same rite but you do something to people by your radiation. Through your field. I have travelled far from where I was then. Next year I will be further still because I am still only beginning to understand the group phenomenon. I have been told that I have to learn it the hard way. And obviously I must be a channel for

Him and He will then work directly rather than me. The first time you talk to the audience you have to first greet the angels, because they are the audience's partners. Tell them, "Please work it out, because I can't." You tell your own angel, "You have to talk to me. I'm your obedient servant." And they are by the way your obedient servants. Then greet the angel of the group, the special angel of the group. Engage him into the game. Then you start, and so it works. I don't go through the parish talking to people about this. The angels do that.

In the morning I call them up and say, please do this, this and that. They say, "Aye sir." And in the evening, please give me a report on what's going on. They prepare a solution. And I say, "Do it," and it's done. You cannot give the angels greater pleasure than to tell them what to do, because their nature is to serve. You tell them what to do so you can do your job better: in praying, being kind, in radiating, and praying in the church. I have the poorest parish in England, an old-folks home with four hundred and twenty people. I've never preached about money. I always get about twenty pounds a week from them without saying a word. Money comes to you when you need it, but I'm not a rich man. I have three hundred pounds in the bank and thirty pounds in the pocket. When I need money, money comes. I said to the angel who is in charge of my finances, "Now look old chap, I don't desire this thing but I have to buy it. Will you provide the money? And money comes. If I concentrated on money I could have millions because it's very easy to gain money. But it is not what I have to do. What should I do with this money? Spend it? Other people are spending money, not me. When I need it, money comes. Thank you, I'll dispose of it. I have a treasurer in the angel, and he knows it. He knows perfectly well when I need it. I am collecting money now for a girl who wants to go to university. So I asked the angel, "Will you help me?" After two months, I've already collected sixty or eighty pounds, so that she has money for next year. I'll get another forty pounds, and every penny is worth it, because she is a bright girl and absolutely dedicated. The angels are wonderful, as are Devas—nature spirits. Peter Caddy at Findhorn will tell you all about them.

Questioner: This thing of manifesting what you need...

AG: Ah, and it *must* be told. Using words.

Questioner: Where is the line, the left side or the right side?

AG: First I have to remove my own blockages because I am often the cause of money not coming. I have my own blockages. I remove blockages and money comes. And to give you an example. You know of Max Freedom Long's, *Secret Science behind Miracles*? The book is about a man who goes to the Polynesian Islands to find out about Kahunas. He stayed there for fifteen years and learned what he could. He has to go back to California. He has a photographic business that is worthwhile and which he wants to sell for seven thousand dollars but he gets an offer of only five hundred for it. The trip itself costs a fortune which he cannot afford. So he goes to his Kahuna, the priest of his local Polynesian village. The priest looks at him and says, "You have done harm to a child, and that is an obstacle for money coming to you." The author says, "What shall I do?" "Go and give a substantial amount of money to a children's cause. A charity. Do penance, that is, try to change the frame of your mind. That is the meaning of penance, not mortification. Change your way of thinking. Then come to me in four weeks time. So he did it. In four weeks time he comes to the Kahuna who looks at him, "The block in your psychology is gone, so there's no obstacle for money to come to you. So you will go next Wednesday to the chap who offered you five hundred dollars, and you will find him at the desk playing with his pencil. You will put the paper in front of him and tell him that you will be back in ten minutes time. He will then offer you seven thousand dollars. So he goes to the office, finds the man at his desk playing with his pencil, and the rest happens exactly as the priest said. He'd removed the blockage, and the money came.

Questioner: I've thought a great deal about this. The trouble is that you don't always have someone to tell you where the blockage is, and also, there may be many more than one. Hundreds of them. It's terribly valuable what you said but it's difficult to...

AG: You don't need to know to know where the blockage is. You need to use your hand. Hold it above a ruler or whatever device you make for detecting the blockage. You'll find one blockage, two three... doesn't matter how many. I just remove them. Gone. And when you remove the blockages, in three or more days time, the money pours in. But, the blockage is in me. Not in other people. I am blocked. When I'm healing, I am often the obstacle, not the patient. We always think, "That I am clear, that I'm a lovely chap, but that one is bad. No, I am bad and that one is probably much better. First clear yourself, and then you'll be able to do that. Very important. Think intensely about yourself as being the obstacle.

Questioner: As you speak, everything is so clear. But what about afterwards?

AG: If you love, you'll get the answer. Because you are in resonance with the problem. And then the problem itself gives you the answer.

But it's always love. Meet any trouble with tremendous love. The trouble then vanishes like fog under the rays of the sun.

Questioner: When you don't have love, how do you regain it?

AG: Love-Light Technique. It comes itself without praying. You cannot force love into you. It's impossible. You can, with your hands, remove blockages against it. But if you practice LLT love comes of itself, without pain, without tears. After a week or two, or perhaps a month, you'll see the difference in you. You'll be amazed at how it happened. The love you find is not the passionate love that attracts you to something. Then you are in resonance with the problem. And when you are in resonance with the problem you know what it is. Somehow you resolve it.

AFTERWORD
MEETING ANDREW GLAZEWSKI—1962

You rarely recognize a life-changing event until long afterwards. For me, meeting Andrew Glazewski during a Lenten retreat proved to be one, though at the time I thought nothing of it. When I was twelve I was sent to Fawley Court, a Polish boarding school run by the Marian Fathers, located in a rambling mansion outside Henley-on-Thames. That was when I first met Andrew.

The Lenten season always elicited a litany of complaints. Each year at Fawley Court, Lent was ushered in by a three day retreat, beginning on Ash Wednesday. That in itself was bad enough—three times a day you had to listen to some priest's one hour sermon, attend Mass in the morning and Mass cum Benediction in the evening. You'd go to confession in between. But worst of all, the retreat shortened a half-term reunion with your parents to no longer than a weekend.

For me that wasn't an issue, as my parents were in Scotland—a ten hour train journey away, so I wouldn't be going away anyway. This was my first year at boarding school. I was coming to terms with the painful, three month separation from home, the only contact with my parents being a weekly letter.

On Ash Wednesday morning Mass was set up in a large drawing room with an alabaster carved ceiling. A row of windows offered a view of the palace grounds. All one hundred and fifty boys along with a few dorm mothers and fathers were crammed in on wooden folding chairs. Altar candles were lit. The warning bell rang, and the altar boys entered along with the priest who was to celebrate Mass. He was a small man, with a wiry body, but despite his diminutive size he radiated a presence that filled the room. You could not ignore him. Most unusual was the square shape of his head, altogether disproportionately large for his body and the tall brow crossed with many wrinkles. His thin grey hair testified to a man in his sixties.

The conversation buzz settled down when he appeared. In a soft but clear voice he intoned *Introibo ad altare Dei*. Mass was sung in Latin. We intoned the responses. At the end of the Mass we lined up. The priest sprinkled ashes on each of our foreheads and said, "Memento homo…" *Remember Man that you are dust and unto dust you will return.*

Most days, breakfast consisted of lumpy porridge with warm milk. You ate it because that's all there was. We had barely enough time to clean up the tables before we had to present ourselves in the drawing room for the first retreat talk. I brought a red notebook and pen.

The unknown priest came in, slowly and apparently in deep thought. He knelt in front of the altar and led us in an Our Father and Hail Mary. But the familiar prayers sounded differently. He spoke slowly as if pausing over each word. You could tell that he was serious about them.

When he stood up and turned to face us, his seriousness vanished. He said that he didn't want to bore us and that if we found him boring, or if he overshot his allotted forty-five minutes to let him know. He wanted us to have a good time.

Throughout his talk a persistent smile hovered on his lips. He had a cocky manner that didn't bow to any authority. While he spoke he kept your attention, not only by what he said but by the cadence of his voice – rising to a pitch when he grew passionate, sometimes barely audible above a whisper. He often used his hands to help make a point. Rather than standing in one place he would pace about, locking eyes with this or that boy.

"So, we're now in Lent," he said. "And they tell you that it's the time to do penance. No doubt you've each made a long list of things to give up for Lent. Your sweets, desserts, anything that you like. So, I'll give up this and give up that. Is there anything left that I can do?" He gave us a penetrating look. "All this giving up of things for Lent is quite fine but it's not penance. It has nothing to do with penance. Penance – the word comes from Greek, "Meta-noia" – changing your way. That's what it's all about. And how do you change your way unless you know what way you are on or where you are going? So, don't give up anything for Lent. You already have enough crosses to bear. Why do you insist on adding to them?"

With considerable relief I scribbled down his words. The advice was certainly fine by me, given that I'd already been feeling guilty about not giving up enough for Lent. Up until now, priests emphasized the virtues of "mortification." They held up as good examples, saints who whipped themselves. You tended to feel guilty unless you were a bit miserable. Or made yourself miserable. Now, here was a priest who asked a reasonable question, "What was the point?"

He told a story. "Take a plank, a foot wide. Can you walk along it? Sure you can. Now have someone blindfold you. Try the plank again. I'm sure you can handle it. Even if your pals lift the plank and set its ends high up, you'll walk along it? But supposing that they remove the blindfold when you're halfway across. I can just see you trying to keep your balance. Even if the plank's a yard across you'll fall off. It's because you tell yourself that you'll fall. We tell ourselves a lot, mostly things about ourselves that aren't true. Then we forget about them. They slip into the subconscious. They're not really forgotten. They influence you whether or not you know about them. Actually, your subconscious is one of your personalities. It has a name, and you can talk to it. Try George; it's as good a name as any. It's important to develop a relationship with George so that you keep him on your side. To help you rather than block you."

After the talk we exchanged our thoughts about the strange priest, Father Andrew Glazewski. I was intrigued by what he said about suggestion, and auto-suggestion, and wanted to find out more. We all wondered when he would get around to talking about God.

The priest anticipated our question. He started off the next talk with, "You probably wonder why I'm not talking about God. Well, I'm not ready to. There are more important things to discuss first. Like the way you talk to George. The messages you tell yourself."

Our beliefs, the messages we tell ourselves are all important. They control our feelings, determine whether we're to be sad or happy. As with the man standing on the high plank, belief can determine our reality. In talking to George, we give ourselves all sorts of messages, constantly and without thinking about them. It's those messages that determine who we are. Who we choose to be. We do have some control over our beliefs.

"It's up to you to choose whether you're going to be happy." After another penetrating look, he said, "What do you want from life? It's the most important question that you can ever ask yourself. The second one is: how are you going to get there?"

I jotted down the questions but I did not understand them. Not until a few years later when I heard him again. George intrigued me because he represented unknown powers. A reader of science fiction, I loved stories of telepathy, people with the ability to fly and so on. George might even make those powers real.

We learned that George has access to all the knowledge of the human race. Especially about everything that has ever happened. At a deeper level, the subconscious is not individual, restricted to me or you, but it is common. It belongs to the entire human race.

I began to understand his drift, when he threw us again. This time by introducing Peter.

"What you're conscious of," he said, "Is a very small part of you. The greatest and most unknown part of you is already in heaven. Aware of God (now he used the word), and living in eternal bliss with God. That is Peter. Your task is to get to know both George and Peter. And you need to work with both. This is important, because people who work exclusively with George eventually find that George takes charge of them. Then they go, you know, cuckoo!"

In later talks he told us more about how to establish a relationship with George. A dowsing pendulum presented one way. He pulled out a wooden bob with a metal bolt through the middle, hanging on a piece of gut. He suggested that we make one and start playing with it, put questions to George and see how he answers them. George can communicate with us through small, scarcely perceptible hand movements, make the pendulum swing this way or that. From working with it we can learn a fair bit about ourselves, the many ways that we've blocked our creative energies, obstacles to pursing the important question—what we want from life.

In between the talks, several of us who were more credulous made our own pendulums and tried them out. For me the pendulum was not new. I'd seen our Rector Father Janicki use one. The occasion was an evening homework session, where our class worked daily, supervised by our dorm mother Zofia Orłowska. Father Andrew Janicki strode in. He was looking for a thief. Theft was not tolerated in the school and resulted in immediate expulsion. A kid was missing some money, and it had clearly been stolen. Father Janicki, a detective to rival Poirot, usually got his man. Hence his nickname, Mousey. Like a mouse he had mysterious ways of sniffing out evildoers. After coming in, he asked us what we knew about the theft. Our class, known for its solidarity in all circumstances, wouldn't give him any information. So, Father Janicki pulled out a pendulum bob and said, "Well, in that case I'll be walking the hallways with my little ball."

After he left, we besieged Mrs. Orłowska with questions about what this was all about. She told us that the Rector had a special ball that turned a certain way when a person he was looking for was standing nearby. He used the ball also for healing work, she said. Many priests have that ability. They can hold their hands over an affected part of the body. The pain goes into their hands. Then they wash the hands, allowing the water to carry away the pain.

Mrs Orłowska was not the sort of person to weave wild stories. She was conservative as they come, more Catholic than the Pope. Later she told us her story, evident in lines of suffering in her face, and hands permanently swollen from frostbite. During the war she and family had been carted off to Siberia where they spent several winters. Later, her young son died from typhoid. Those experiences explained her toughness. Her implacability. And yet, when you came to her alone she'd be as sweet as a caring mother. Her endorsement of Father Janicki's pendulum and healing hands meant something.

The following week I saw Father Janicki walking with his pendulum bob down a hallway. Soon afterward, one of the boys was expelled. We never learned whether the pendulum played any part in discovering the boy.

One evening I watched Father Janicki remove a friend's headache. They were standing in a corner of the assembly hall where lots of kids were milling about. The priest moved his hands in a circular movement in the space above my friend's head, stopped occasionally to shake his hands. Finally he asked, "Is it gone?" Apparently it was gone. He wasn't the only one. Father Paul Jasinski, the Father Superior also was a practitioner whom I discovered, working on a boy's head and back. Soon several of us tried out on each other a simple exercise of holding up our hands with palms facing each other, to see whether we could feel anything. After a few tries, I could sense little pinpricks that varied when my partner moved his hands in circles. Something was definitely happening there.

About midway through the retreat, Andrew talked to us about prayer. But not a whole lot about God, at least the way we expected him to.

"If prayer is a conversation," he said, "Doesn't that involve two way communication? What sort of conversation is it where you're talking the whole time, begging for something or other? If you want a true conversation with God, don't you think that you should shut up and let God speak to you? The first requirement for prayer is silence. To listen, listen—and then to listen."

So how do you pray? He introduced us to what he later called, the Prayer of Light. You imagine yourself lying on a beach with the sun shining on you, its rays warming you.

"The sun is the source of all light, warmth and energy. Feel its warmth all over you, on every part of your skin. Move this way and that so that the light warms every part of you. It's easy to do this with the real sun, and that's the way to begin. You don't need any words for this sort of prayer. You aren't saying anything or asking for anything, only feeling the sun's warmth. After a while, you'll come to see that you actually carry that sun inside you. Turn your attention to that light, and let it penetrate your entire body, arms legs, all the way to your fingertips. Feel it, as strongly as you can. Use all your imagination to make it real, to draw the light into yourself. This must be repeated many times a day, opening yourself completely to His power so he Himself can take charge of you. You'll find out that not only you're a carrier of this light, but that you can share it with others."

After the talk I tried out his prayer. So did a few friends with whom I compared notes, but we all found the exercise difficult. How do you imagine a sun without using any words? Was the Prayer of Light even a prayer, at least the way that we'd been conditioned to believe? Andrew knew that this aspect of his teaching would be the most difficult, but he also felt that it was the most important because he returned to it in subsequent talks. He understood that many of us found his approach difficult, but he urged us not to get discouraged but to keep working at it. That the more often we practised it the easier it would become. "The penny will drop".

When I came home, I shared Andrew's teachings with my parents. They couldn't make anything of them. I tried to explain the Prayer of Light, but my mother, try as she might, couldn't figure out what I was saying. My father thought that the pendulum was pretty fishy. I soon realized, to my astonishment, that the mysterious world that Andrew talked about was unknown in the greater world outside Fawley Court. But why not? The Marian Fathers were a conservative bastion of the Catholic Church. Fawley Court was not a place where you could de-bate or question a point of doctrine. If what Andrew taught us wasn't heretical, why wasn't it more widely known?

If I hadn't met Andrew again, I probably would have forgotten his message after a few years. Though George and Peter sounded interesting, they remained largely theoretical. The Prayer of Light was a lot of work, and so I put it away along with other stuff I couldn't wrap my mind about.

Three years later, Andrew returned to lead another retreat. By that time I was ready for his message.

NOTES

Foreword

(1) Information on Andrew's early years is based on Bob Bloomfield's 1995 unpublished monograph, "Andrew Glazewski – The Psychic Priest", and on taped conversations between Bloomfield and Andrew's brother, Konstanty.

(2) Bruce MacManaway and Joanna Turcan, *Healing, the energy that can restore health*, 1983, Thorsons, 128pp

Chapter 1 — The Science Behind Healing

(1) A talk to Edinburgh University students, November 1968

(2) Lviv, in Ukraine

(3) Hans Speeman, *Embryonic Development and Induction* 1938, Yale University Press, 401 pp.

(4) Harold Saxton Burr and F. S. C. Northop, *Evidence for the Existence of an Electro-dynamic field in Living Organisms*, Proc. Nat Acad Sci 25, No 6, 284-288 1939

(5) One millionth of a meter

(6) A. J. K. Glazewski, *The Gravitational Wave*, Proceedings of the Scientific and Technical Congress of Radionics and Radiesthesia, held in London, May 1950.

(7) Stanley Backster referred to Cleve Backster's work, described further in *The Secret Life of Plants* by Peter Tompkins and Christopher Bird, 1974.

(8) By comparison, a GPS signal has a strength of a millionth of a Watt, about the same magnitude as the random movement of air molecules. It can be detected because of its recognizable pattern.

(9) Gustaf Stromberg, *Emergent Energy* Journal of the Franklin Institute, 1946, v. 241, Issue 5, p 323–339.

(10) Gustaf Stromberg, *The Autonomous Field*, 1945, Journal of the Franklin Institute, v. 239, no. 1, p27-40.

(11) Andrew was then with the Polish army, stationed in Germany.

(12) Available in English from the Sacred Science Institute (hanskayser.com) as *Textbook of Harmonics*.

(13) Maxwell Maltz, *Psychocybernetics*, 1960, Psychocybernetics Foundation, 292 pp.

Chapter 2 — Angels

(1) A Conversation between Andrew Glazewski and Bruce MacManaway at the Westbank Healing Centre, Strathmiglo, Nov 26, 1969

(2) Here Andrew follows the language of astronomer and physicist Gustaf Stromberg, who classified human fields as Primary or Secondary. The Secondary Field consists of physical fields such as electromagnetic, sound and infra red. The Primary Field enfolds those and may involve higher dimensions than space and time. A non-local field, its properties resemble the Morphogenetic Field of Rupert Sheldrake and the Akashik field of Ervin Laszlo.

(3) See Aquinas's, "Summa Theologicae – De Angeli". Aquinas bases much of his teaching on Angels on the works of the sixth century Neo-platonic philosopher Dionysius the Areopagite.

(4) As discussed in Chapter 11, a closed system is one that does not exchange energy with its surroundings but is self-contained. An astronaut taking a spacewalk is a closed system. He/she cannot move except by pushing against an external object.

(5) Most probably the Cottingley fairies described by Sir Arthur Conan Doyle in "The Coming of the Fairies" 1920.

Chapter 3 — The Mechanics of Prayer

(1) Talk given around 1966 at an unknown location.

Chapter 4 — Touching the Divine

(1) A Conversation between Andrew Glazewski, Bruce MacManaway and members of a healing group, held at the Westbank Centre, Strathmiglo, Nov 26, 1969

Chapter 5 — Love, Marriage and Sex

(1) Conversation with a healing group at the Westbank Centre, November 1968

(2) "The Human Jungle" 60 episodes were first shown on BBC television, 1963-1964.

(3) Rudolf von Urban (1879-1964) was to have been a priest when, after meeting Sigmund Freud, he studied medicine and became a psychologist, specializing in the study of sexuality. He wrote "Sex Perfection" in 1952, published by Rider & Co.

Chapter 6 — Meditation

(1) Recorded by two friends in 1971. Reprinted with permission from the Wrekin Trust.

Chapter 7 — The Holy Trinity

(1) Talk to a healing group at Westbank Healing Centre, Nov 26, 1969.

(2) Though Andrew uses the masculine pronoun to refer to God, it's clear that no gender is implied. God as a Field is neither masculine nor feminine.

(3) Early Christian literature refers to this relationship as *emanation*. "Procession" is the equivalent word derived from Latin.

Chapter 8 — The Name of God

(1) Recorded by two friends in 1971. Reprinted with permission from the Wrekin Trust.

(2) Gospel of Thomas, Log 3 – "The Kingdom is within you and it is without you."

Chapter 9 — The Eucharist

(1) Recorded by two friends in 1971. Reprinted with permission from the Wrekin Trust.

Chapter 10 — Developing Field Awareness

(1) Talk at Westbank Centre, Strathmiglo November 1969

(2) Hans Speeman, *Embryonic Development and Induction* 1938, Yale University Press, 401 pp.

Chapter 11 — What happens when we die?

(1) Talk at Westbank Healing Centre, November 1968

(2) The implication is that after death the Primary Field no longer develops because it is a closed physical system. Though it contains many levels that are accessible to us, depending on our level of awareness, we no longer grow in consciousness as when we were able to refer to our body.

(3) Sirius B— a white dwarf star.

Chapter 12 — The Practice of Group Healing

(1) A dialog with Bruce and Patricia MacManaway, November 1968

Chapter 13 — The Healing Hand

(1) Reprinted and edited. Original paper was published in *The London Hospital Gazette*, April 1967 under the title, "Can there be any science behind healing hands?"

(2) A. J. K. Glazewski, *The Gravitational Wave*, Proceedings of the Scientific and Technical Congress of Radionics and Radiesthesia, held in London, May 1950., ref. 4 at the end.

(3) J. C. Bose, All his works, though mainly *Comparative Electrophysiology* Longmans Green, 1907.

(4) H. Schaeffer, *Electrophysiologie*, Book 1, Algemine Physiologic , 1940, p. 229, 418. Also, K. S. Cole, *Permeability and impermeability of cell membranes for ions*, Cold Spring Harbour Symp,1940, 8, p 110.

(5) H. S. Burr, *Field properties of the developing Frog's Egg*, Proc. Nat. Acad. Science, 1941, 27, p 276.

(6) W. G. Cady, *Piezoelectricity*, McGraw-Hill, 1946. For electrostriction see pp. 4, 198-99, 614.

(7) Hans Selye, *The Story of the Adaptation Syndrome,* Montreal, Aeta, Inc., 1952

(8) J. Gershon-Cohen, *Medical Thermography,* Scientific American, (Feb. 1967) pp. 94 ssq.

(9) G. T. Fechner, *Elements der Psychophysic,* 1860. See also Encyclopaedia Britannica, under Fechner.

Chapter 14 — The Music of Crystals, Plants and Human Beings

(1) Reprinted and edited. Original paper was published in Radio Perception September 1951. This paper contains the most detailed discussion of the physics underlying the sonic and electric fields. It represents the writer's early explorations, and gives some insight into his experimental work. He later developed this theory to include Gustav Stromberg's Primary and Secondary fields.

(2) J. Tyndall : *Sound,* Longmans Green, London, 1898 p. 41

(3) H. Kayser, *Der Hörende Mensch. Elemente eines Akustischen Weltbildes,* Lambert Schneider, Berlin, 1932, chap. 2, *Zahlgestalt der Harmonik,* pp 95 ssq.

(4) See G. T. Fehner: *Elemente der Psychophysik,* Leipzig, 1889, compare H. Kayser: *Lehrbuch der Harmonik,* Occidentverlag, Zurich, 1950, p. 45 ssq.

(5) C. H. Weiss in the Abhandlungen der Akademie zu Berlin, 1818-1819 *Physikalisehe Klasse* quoted after H. Kayser. *Der Horende* Mensch, p. 123, ref. 2

(6) V. Goldschmidt, *Ober Harmonic und Komplikation,* Berlin, 1901

(7) H. Kayser: *Vom Kiang der Welt,* Oecidentverlag, Zurich, 1946, pp. 88-89; see also H. Kayser, *Der Horende Mensch* as above, chap. III, *Vom klang in Anorganischen,* 2 Kristalographie, p. 159 ssq, and *Lehrbuch der Harmonik,* as above, pp. 65, 93, 229, 267

(8) L. Bragg, *The Crystalline State*, Bell, London, 1949, plate XXIX, patterns of mica and rock salts

(9) J. C. Bose, *Response in the Living and Non-Living*, Longmans Green, London, 1922. See also J. C. Bose, *Comparative Electro-physiology*, Longmans Green, London, 1907, and other works by the same author

(10) E. Ludin, *Metal Wires Electrically Heated and Producing Sounds* (translation), Archives Des Sciences Physiques et Naturels I, IV, p. 383, 1922. See also F. Streintz, Physikalicshe Zeitschr. 16, p137, 1915, and A. Imhof, Physik. Zeitschr. 23, p26, 1922

(11) It may be objected—as Ludin does—that longitudinal vibrations in wires are entirely excluded. This is only partly correct. The molecules of the heated wire try to vibrate along the direction of the electric field. As this is actually to a great extent hindered, their vibration will result in the direction permissible by the conditions. The following experiment which demonstrates this was from Young. "He allowed a sheet of sunlight, to cross a pianoforte wire, and obtained thus a brilliant dot. Striking the wire he caused it to vibrate, the dot described a luminous line like that produced by the whirling of a burning coal in the air, and the form of this line revealed the character of the vibration. It was rendered manifest by these experiments that the oscillations of the wire were not confined to a single plane, but that it described in its vibrations curves of greater or less complexity. Superimposed upon the vibration of the whole string were partial vibrations, which revealed themselves as loops and sinuosities. Every one of these figures corresponds to a distinct impression made by the wire upon the surrounding air" (from J. Tyndall, op. cit., P. 121). Actually it can be shown, that any transversely vibrating wire fixed at its ends, will produce at these ends a stress-strain reaction, which in its turn will tend to produce a longitudinally vibrating component along the wire, resulting in a standing wave. Young's experiment partly reproduces this effect. Thus, it is believed, the meaning of the above diagram is explained. The full mathematical treatment and the discussion between Young and Fresnel can be found in the works of Poisson. See also Prof. T.J.J., "The New Theory of the Aether," Astron. Nadir. No. 5085, vol. 212, Feb., 1921, where the Poisson discussion is treated at. length. Mutatis mutandis it, can be applied to our case.

(12) See papers by Felix Ehrenhaft on photophoresis, the interaction of electromagnetic and mechanical waves, such as *Photophoresis and Its Interpretation by Electric and Magnetic Ions*, Journal of the Franklin Institute, vol 233 (March 1942), pp. 235–255.

(13) *Baron von Reichenbach's Experiments*, The Journal of Borderland Research, Vol. 54, No. 2, 2nd Quarter 1998

(14) H. Kayser, *Harmonia Plantarum*, Benno Schwabe, Basel, 1943

(15) H. Kayser, *Harmonia Plantarum*, Benno Schwabe, Basel, pp. 70-71

(16) The works quoted here above

(17) From Discovery, May, 1951, Vol. XII, No. 5, p. 152

(18) A. Glazewski, *The Gravitational Wave*, Proceedings of the Scientific and Technical Congress of Radionics and Radiesthesia, London, May, 1950. Published by the Committee of the Congress, pp. 112 ssq. See also T.J.J. The *New Theory of the Aether* Astron. Nachr., No. 5085, Vol. 212, Feb., 1921, and E. G. Cullwick, *An Anomaly in Electro-magnetic Theory*, Nature, Vol. 161, p. 969, Jan. 19th, 1948

(19) J. Tyndall, work quoted above, pp. 276-278

(20) J. W. S. Rayleigh: *The Theory of Sound*, Macmillan, London, 1896, Vol. II, p. 369. The proposed explanation by Beetz given there does not conform with the reaction of jets to magnetic fields. This was not known to Beetz

(21) A. Glazewski, *The Gravitational Wave*, as above, p. 14, note 10

(22) W. E. Benham: *The Nature of Temperature*, Proc. Phys. Soc., Vol. LIV, p. 121, 1942 Benham explores the nature of temperature per se. He argues that temperature is related to the amplitude of an electromagnetic wave, the view also expressed by the writer.

(23) See interesting note of M. F. Perutz, *Submicroscopic Structure of the Red Cell*, Nature, Vol. 161, p. 204, Feb. 7th, 1948

Chapter 15 — The Pattern of Telepathic Communication

(1) Edited from a talk given to the Annual Conference of the Radionic Association, 1973.

(2) The Lviv Lemberg Technical University. See page 147.

(3) A Gurwitsch, *A historical review of the problem of mitogenetic radiation*, Experientia, 1988, 44, pp545-50.

(4) H. Burr, *Electrodynamic Theory of Life*, Quarterly Review of Biology,10(3), p 322, 1935.

(5) Gustaf Stromberg, *The Autonomous Field*, 1945, Journal of the Franklin Institute, v. 239, no. 1, p27-40.

(6) R. Wilhelm & C. G. Jung, *The Secret of the Golden Flower*, Routledge & Kegan Paul p. 21. Reprint 1989.

(7) Peter Tompkins and Christopher Bird, *The Secret Life of Plants*, 416pp, 1973

(8) Andrew taught this approach 1972-1973 to small groups, usually in a natural setting, such as in his summer workshops on the Scillies. In Chapter 16 he describes the technique in more detail.

BIBLIOGRAPHY

"The Gravitational Wave,", Proceedings of the Scientific and Technical Congress of Radionics and Radiesthesia, London, May, 1950.

"The Music of Crystals, Plants and Human Beings", Radio Perception, September 1951

"A New Suspension of the Magnetic Needle", Radio Perception Vol XI, 80, June 1953

"Miłość" (Love) Summa Theologica by Thomas Aquinas Volume 16, Translated into Polish with Commentary, Veritas, 1960.

"Can there be any science behind Healing Hands?" The London Hospital Gazette, March 1967.

"The Human Field in Medical Problems", Psionic Medicine, 1970

"The Pattern of Telepathic Communication", The Radionic Association, 1974.

"The Mechanics of Prayer", The Wrekin Trust, 1974.

"Andrew Glazewski—The Psychic Priest" by Bob Bloomfield, Unpublished monograph, 1995.

Paperbacks also available from
White Crow Books

Elsa Barker—*Letters from
a Living Dead Man*
ISBN 978-1-907355-83-7

Elsa Barker—*War Letters from
the Living Dead Man*
ISBN 978-1-907355-85-1

Elsa Barker—*Last Letters from
the Living Dead Man*
ISBN 978-1-907355-87-5

Richard Maurice Bucke—
Cosmic Consciousness
ISBN 978-1-907355-10-3

Arthur Conan Doyle—
The Edge of the Unknown
ISBN 978-1-907355-14-1

Arthur Conan Doyle—
The New Revelation
ISBN 978-1-907355-12-7

Arthur Conan Doyle—
The Vital Message
ISBN 978-1-907355-13-4

Arthur Conan Doyle with
Simon Parke—*Conversations
with Arthur Conan Doyle*
ISBN 978-1-907355-80-6

Meister Eckhart with Simon Parke—
Conversations with Meister Eckhart
ISBN 978-1-907355-18-9

D. D. Home—*Incidents in my Life Part 1*
ISBN 978-1-907355-15-8

Mme. Dunglas Home; edited,
with an Introduction, by Sir
Arthur Conan Doyle—*D. D.
Home: His Life and Mission*
ISBN 978-1-907355-16-5

Edward C. Randall—
Frontiers of the Afterlife
ISBN 978-1-907355-30-1

Rebecca Ruter Springer—
Intra Muros: My Dream of Heaven
ISBN 978-1-907355-11-0

Leo Tolstoy, edited by Simon
Parke—*Forbidden Words*
ISBN 978-1-907355-00-4

Leo Tolstoy—*A Confession*
ISBN 978-1-907355-24-0

Leo Tolstoy—*The Gospel in Brief*
ISBN 978-1-907355-22-6

Leo Tolstoy—*The Kingdom
of God is Within You*
ISBN 978-1-907355-27-1

Leo Tolstoy—*My Religion:
What I Believe*
ISBN 978-1-907355-23-3

Leo Tolstoy—*On Life*
ISBN 978-1-907355-91-2

Leo Tolstoy—*Twenty-three Tales*
ISBN 978-1-907355-29-5

Leo Tolstoy—*What is Religion
and other writings*
ISBN 978-1-907355-28-8

Leo Tolstoy—*Work While
Ye Have the Light*
ISBN 978-1-907355-26-4

Leo Tolstoy—*The Death of Ivan Ilyich*
ISBN 978-1-907661-10-5

Leo Tolstoy—*Resurrection*
ISBN 978-1-907661-09-9

Leo Tolstoy with Simon Parke—
Conversations with Tolstoy
ISBN 978-1-907355-25-7

Howard Williams with an Introduction
by Leo Tolstoy—*The Ethics of Diet:
An Anthology of Vegetarian Thought*
ISBN 978-1-907355-21-9

Vincent Van Gogh with Simon
Parke—*Conversations with Van Gogh*
ISBN 978-1-907355-95-0

Wolfgang Amadeus Mozart with Simon
Parke—*Conversations with Mozart*
ISBN 978-1-907661-38-9

Jesus of Nazareth with Simon Parke—
Conversations with Jesus of Nazareth
ISBN 978-1-907661-41-9

Thomas à Kempis with Simon
Parke—*The Imitation of Christ*
ISBN 978-1-907661-58-7

Julian of Norwich with Simon
Parke—*Revelations of Divine Love*
ISBN 978-1-907661-88-4

Allan Kardec—*The Spirits Book*
ISBN 978-1-907355-98-1

Allan Kardec—*The Book on Mediums*
ISBN 978-1-907661-75-4

Emanuel Swedenborg—*Heaven and Hell*
ISBN 978-1-907661-55-6

P.D. Ouspensky—*Tertium Organum:
The Third Canon of Thought*
ISBN 978-1-907661-47-1

Dwight Goddard—*A Buddhist Bible*
ISBN 978-1-907661-44-0

Michael Tymn—*The Afterlife Revealed*
ISBN 978-1-970661-90-7

Michael Tymn—*Transcending the
Titanic: Beyond Death's Door*
ISBN 978-1-908733-02-3

Guy L. Playfair—*If This Be Magic*
ISBN 978-1-907661-84-6

Guy L. Playfair—*The Flying Cow*
ISBN 978-1-907661-94-5

Guy L. Playfair —*This House is Haunted*
ISBN 978-1-907661-78-5

Carl Wickland, M.D.—
Thirty Years Among the Dead
ISBN 978-1-907661-72-3

John E. Mack—*Passport to the Cosmos*
ISBN 978-1-907661-81-5

Peter & Elizabeth Fenwick—
The Truth in the Light
ISBN 978-1-908733-08-5

Erlendur Haraldsson—
Modern Miracles
ISBN 978-1-908733-25-2

Erlendur Haraldsson—
At the Hour of Death
ISBN 978-1-908733-27-6

Erlendur Haraldsson—
The Departed Among the Living
ISBN 978-1-908733-29-0

Brian Inglis—*Science and Parascience*
ISBN 978-1-908733-18-4

Brian Inglis—*Natural and Supernatural:
A History of the Paranormal*
ISBN 978-1-908733-20-7

Ernest Holmes—*The Science of Mind*
ISBN 978-1-908733-10-8

Victor & Wendy Zammit —*A Lawyer
Presents the Evidence For the Afterlife*
ISBN 978-1-908733-22-1

Casper S. Yost—*Patience
Worth: A Psychic Mystery*
ISBN 978-1-908733-06-1

William Usborne Moore—
Glimpses of the Next State
ISBN 978-1-907661-01-3

William Usborne Moore—
The Voices
ISBN 978-1-908733-04-7

John W. White—
The Highest State of Consciousness
ISBN 978-1-908733-31-3

Stafford Betty—
The Imprisoned Splendor
ISBN 978-1-907661-98-3

Paul Pearsall, Ph.D. —
Super Joy
ISBN 978-1-908733-16-0

All titles available as eBooks, and selected titles available in Hardback and Audiobook formats from www.whitecrowbooks.com